Building Character

With God's Laws And Declarations

E. Dale Click

CSS Publishing Company, Inc., Lima, Ohio

BUILDING CHARACTER

Copyright © 2004 by
CSS Publishing Company, Inc.
Lima, Ohio

All rights reserved. No part of this publication may be reproduced in any manner whatsoever without the prior permission of the publisher, except in the case of brief quotations embodied in critical articles and reviews. Inquiries should be addressed to: Permissions, CSS Publishing Company, Inc., P.O. Box 4503, Lima, Ohio 45802-4503.

Scripture quotations are from the *New Revised Standard Version of the Bible*, copyright 1989 by the Division of Christian Education of the National Council of the Churches of Christ in the USA. Used by permission.

For more information about CSS Publishing Company resources, visit our website at www.csspub.com or e-mail us at custserv@csspub.com or call (800) 241-4056.

ISBN 0-7880-2308-X   PRINTED IN U.S.A.

To People Of Character:

*My sister, Pauline, and
her deceased husband, Wilson Matthews,
and their son and his wife
The Reverend Larry W. Matthews and Nancy*

Table Of Contents

Introduction 7

Part One: Laws
- I. Monotheism 9
- II. Respect 15
- III. Honor 23
- IV. Chastity And Fairness 31
- V. Truthfulness 37
- VI. Neighborliness 43

Part Two: Declarations
- VII. Kingdom People 49
- VIII. Brokenhearted People 55
- IX. Disciplined People 61
- X. Righteous People 67
- XI. Kindhearted People 73
- XII. Pure-In-Heart People 79
- XIII. Peacemaker People 85

Introduction

Character is an elusive word. It is used in describing the content of a person. Athletes use it: "Guys with character usually show it when adversity is at hand, when there are obstacles that are great" (Laker backup center, John Salley, *Los Angeles Times*, May 26, 2000). It is doubtful former President Ronald Reagan's statement is to be taken seriously: "You can tell a lot about a fellow's character by his way of eating jelly beans" (*New York Times*, January 15, 1981). But, you can tell a lot about people by the way they regard God's laws. And, you can tell a lot about people by their declarations about life.

Our country is in a character crisis. A former president of these United States faced disbarment proceedings. Millionaire athletes lose their livelihood and land in jail. A movie star with a bad temper rages out of control and operates on the premise that stardom merits freedom to abuse people. A church executive of a national organization misuses funds. The list is frightening. Even one of my catechetical students lied when confronted about missing class, claiming illness, when in fact his father had reported he slept in that Sunday morning. The character of our country is showing and it is not a matter of how we eat jelly beans. It is a matter of how we look upon God's laws and declarations.

God's laws are timeless and timely. Regardless of your religion, race, or age, if you ignore or break any of the ten commandments, you are headed for trouble.

Astoundingly, countless people look upon life as a puzzle. Their simple theory seems to be: fit together the four *outer* edges of a puzzle (life) — 1) get an education; 2) get a job; 3) get a gal or a guy; and, 4) get a television set — mistakenly concluding other pieces of life will fit. Life is not a puzzle. It is not a matter of fitting pieces together until you get the right formula. It is a matter of putting God in the center of life as Jesus recommended: "... Strive first for the kingdom of God and his righteousness, and all these things will be given to you as well" (Matthew 6:33). Put God smack in the center of life and the pieces of life fit together naturally. You don't even have to figure it out. God has figured it by providing commandments and declarations. People living on the perimeter live unnaturally.

Add Jesus' declarations/beatitudes and you will enjoy life, naturally. It is surprising how initially the beatitudes look unnatural. Further examination reveals qualities of life that build character.

Saint Paul simplified a succession of statements that make sense, in Romans 5: "... that suffering produces endurance, and endurance produces character, and character produces hope, and hope does not disappoint us."

It is my earnest hope that these summations of God's laws and descriptions of Jesus' declarations in the beatitudes will help someone in this matter of character building.

Part One: Laws

I. Monotheism

No matter how many people teach you to go contrary to this first commandment, dismiss them and say, I must fear and trust God more than you. Then they will become fine people; otherwise they will grow up to be blockheads. The chief part of all wisdom and knowledge is the first commandment, namely, that you should fear and trust no one but God alone. He will richly reward you. In the course of time you will learn to apply it well in every situation and action (Luther's Works, American Edition, Volume 51, p. 141).

The First Commandment: "I am the Lord your God, who rescued you from Egypt, where you were slaves. Worship no God but me" (Exodus 20:2-3; Deuteronomy 5:6-7).

The voice of Alexandre Gustav Eiffel (1832-1923), a French engineer, could be heard from the tower he built in Paris in 1889 for the Exposition, a tower which housed the French wireless telegraphic service. "This famed tower is 984 feet high, of iron framework supported by four masonry piers on a base 330 feet square, from which rise four columns to 620 feet where they unite in one shaft" (*The Columbia Encyclopedia in One Volume*, p. 555). The Eiffel Tower stands today as one of the great engineering feats of all time. From the top platform the view can be seen for 85 miles. Elevators shoot up to the three platforms. I chose to walk to the top. In 1889 Alexandre Gustav Eiffel's voice could be heard from that tower.

The voice that spoke from Mount Sinai some 3,000 years ago still reverberates in all lands. Ten statements, so brief and complete, so intertwining morality and religion, so free from national peculiarities, so close fitting to fundamental duties, are authoritative for many peoples of the world.

From the top of Mount Sinai came a view of God's relationship to humankind, humankind's relationship to God, and humankind's relationship to one another — a telegraphic view which will last as long as civilization. "God spoke, and these were his words ..." (Exodus 20:1).

The engineering secret of the Eiffel Tower is its four masonry piers on a base of 330 feet square. From this base the columns rise.

The strength of the commandments is its base: "I am the Lord your God ... Worship no God but me." From this base rise the columns of commandments.

It is noteworthy that the Old Testament never concerned itself with atheism; it is concerned with idolatry, the worship of false gods.

We think of an idol or false god as the worship of something conceived as personality, perhaps resident in a stone or a pole or a statue. In primitive religions idols represented more than this. The figure or image represented a hope or an aspiration of a person. For example, the gods of the Canaanites were the fertility gods, Baalism. The highest value in their culture was fertility, whether of animals or crops or people.

Sometimes idolatry in primitive times was predominantly monotheistic; that is, there was one value considered as the top god, although other gods were recognized as exciting.

People in the new millennium have the same problem as primitive people: the difficulty of determining which is the top god. This remains the problem of humankind until the basis of belief has been defined. The recognition of the existence of other gods has pulled the rug from under humankind's theological feet.

Moses gave the word of God to his people: "I am the Lord your God. You shall have no other gods." God is the creator; he is the basis of all. He is the fountain of life. Everything has relationship to him. If people are made by God, if they are the image of God, they cannot become what they are meant to be if they ignore God, if they deny God, if they defy their structural God-relationship.

People come from God. If a person's life repudiates God, he or she no longer has life. This is what Paul declared when he said,

"For the wages of sin is death ..." (Romans 6:23). A person's life bears fruit, a person's life blooms when there is connection to the base. This is monotheism — belief in one God.

Luther's catechism urges us to "fear, love, and trust in God above anything else."

On the three platforms at varying heights of the Eiffel Tower are guardrails to prevent accidents. Without them, I would not have been able to climb to the various platforms.

The commandments guard us along the ascent and descent of life. Disregarding any commandment invites disaster.

Not everybody fears God. There is fear of misfortune, fear of losing money, fear of losing health, fear of certain personalities; there is national fear of another culture that might crush us. But, have you heard anyone admit fear in not worshiping God? Afraid of not remembering or ignoring the commandments? Afraid of God? We have watered down this word "fear" by saying it means only respect. Where is the awe in worship? Where is the tiptoe religion of today? Where is the sense of expectancy? Sodom and Gomorrah could not have been more impervious to the presence of God than the general populace of our day.

The first commandment requires fearing no one and trusting no one except God alone. Moses told his people to write the commandments upon walls, to bind them upon their wrists (phylacteries), and to keep them before their eyes. But, it must go further than that. This commandment must be applied.

When a wrong is committed, a person needs not only to fear the circumstance or the consequence, but to fear God, because you are God's person. Commandments require discipline. If you are to cease from doing evil, you must fear and trust God. Thus, for God's sake you cease evil. It is because of your love for God, you cease evil. It is because of your trust in God above everything that you cease evil. If you are afraid of trusting and loving God, you do not fear God. You live in a vacuum of vanity. You live on a foundation that will crumble with your ashes.

Martin Luther (1483-1546) said, "All the wisdom which is in the Scriptures follow from the first commandment" (*Luther's*

Works, op. cit., p. 140). David boasted in Psalm 119:100: "I understand more than the aged, for I keep your precepts." Jesus made it plain: "But strive first for the kingdom of God and his righteousness, and all these things will be given to you as well" (Matthew 6:33). To the church in Rome Paul wrote: "I appeal to you therefore, brothers and sisters, to present your bodies as a living sacrifice, holy and acceptable to God, which is your spiritual worship." Paul continued, "Do not be conformed to this world, but be transformed by the renewing of your minds, so that you will discern the will of God — what is good and acceptable and perfect" (Romans 12:1-2).

When the commandments grip us, so does God, and we become enraptured by his will. What is good and acceptable and perfect? "You shall love the Lord your God with all your heart, and with all your soul, and with all your mind (might)" (Deuteronomy 6:5; Matthew 22:37).

There is a marked difference between morality and Christianity. Morality can dress up in religion. You can build a theory of ethics from a base of self-righteousness. You can be moral without being monotheistic. You can be good without God. If the base of your goodness is a mate, or a position, or an inheritance, or intelligence, or self-sufficiency, such goodness without reference to God is condemned by the deeper and simpler wisdom of God who was "... in Christ ... reconciling the world to him ..." (2 Corinthians 5:19). "So if anyone is in Christ, there is a new creation: everything old has passed away ... everything has become new!" (2 Corinthians 5:17).

Christians need to refresh their memories with this lesson. The commandments were born in a world with the strong temptation to polytheism, with which the Israelites struggled for years. People around them believed in many gods. Egypt swarmed with them. Abraham's faith was sadly tarnished in his sons. Nevertheless, monotheism laid the very foundation for Israel's national life. Monotheism determined its history.

This first commandment is more of a revelation than a mere command. It is a declaration that at the center of all, God is enthroned. There is one ultimate *cause* on which all rests. The heart cannot pour out its love when it is shared by many.

A poet exclaimed, "Only when a lost soul sees in Christ the God of all souls, does it fold its wings and rest as a bird after a long flight." Thomas Paine (1737-1809), American political theorist, writer, and a Quaker, confessed, "I believe in one God and no more ..." (*The Age of Reason*, pt. 1, 1793).

This commandment teaches us to surrender life to one God. The first commandment is a prelude to the worship of God in Christ, the motivation to entrust all to our Maker and Redeemer. Christ's journey to the cross is most precious to believers. Christ made the greatest sacrifice. He draws our warmest love. Without Christ we are desolate. With Christ we are blessed. In Christ we see commandments fulfilled.

The commandments require obedience. Obedience is the candle which lights up this new millennium. Faith is the hand that takes ours and gives us light for the leading of the mind, heart, will, affections, hopes, and fears. Character is built.

II. Respect

The Second Commandment: "You shall not take the name of the Lord your God in vain."
"What does this mean for us? We are to fear and love God so that we do not use his name to curse, swear, lie, or deceive, but call on him in prayer, praise, and thanksgiving."

Names mean something. As a lad, I was always fascinated by Indian names. Where did they get such names as Eagle Eye, Buffalo Face, Sitting Bull, Sleepy Eye, and Rain-in-the-Face? I learned that American Indian fathers chose names from the first object that caught their eye after a child's birth.

Throughout history, names have been given to people (*The World Book Encyclopedia*, Volume 12, pp. 5,385-5,386). Early history records only one name used since there were fewer people. As communities grew and people moved about, there were not enough names to go around.

Among Christians, a name was given at baptism and became known as the Christian or given name. John was a popular name. If there was more than one, they became known as, for example, *Peter's son* or *Jack's son*. Some were known for their job or profession, such as *John the Carpenter* or *John the Shepherd*. *John Long* was a tall man; *John Short* was a short man. Or, after people traveled around, *John from the North*, or *John the Scot*.

Names added were nicknames. Eventually, they became family names. People who owned land made up names. For example, in Germany, the name of von Hindenburg means from *Hidden Castle*. The French name de Chateubriand means from *Briand Castle*.

In early days not all people could read or write. Names were made up. The name of *Sanderson* came from Alexander's son and *Michael* became Mitchell. The old name *ap-Hugh*, a Welsh name, meaning the *son* was changed to Pugh. The names of Fitzhugh

15

and McCue were once the same, both meaning the *son of Hugh*. Still other names, like the Indians, came from objects: Lake, Stone, Clay, Woods, and Appling.

Surnames (added names), formed from the father's name, came from other languages. For example, the *son of* include Irish names beginning with O; German names ending in *sohn* or *son*; Scandinavian names ending in *sen* or *son*; Russian and Serbian names ending *ovitch* and *escu*. So we get such names as Johnson, Johansson, Hansen, Ivanovitch, and Jonescu.

The first use of Christian names began in England in the 1500s. Such names include Dudley, Sidney, Washington, Chauncey, Clifford, Howard, Russell, Spencer, and Tracy.

In early times, only nobles and people of wealth used more than one Christian name. But in the 1500s, two Christian names became common. The Roman Catholic Church is credited for this, naming children after a saint, for example. The second name is used for family reasons. A girl born at Liverpool, England, in 1880, was given 25 Christian names after all the letters in the alphabet. She was called Anna Bertha Cecilia Diana Emily Fanny Gertrude Hypatia Inez Jane Kate Louise Maud Nora Ophelia Quince Rebecca Starkey Teresa Ulysis Venus Winfred Xenophone Yetty Zero *Pepper*.

Hebrew boys were given names with a definite meaning: Isaac (laughter); Solomon (prince of peace); Nathan (gift); Samuel (called of God); Zachary (Jehovah has remembered). Some common Hebrew girl names were Susan (lily); Rachel (ewe); Elizabeth (consecrated of God). The names of John and Joan are both Hebrew words meaning God is gracious.

In the New Testament, Jesus gave Peter a new name (rock). I don't think they called him "Rocky," however! Peter in French is Pierre; in Italy, Pietro; and in Spain, Pedro.

Many names from ancient Greece are used: Nicholas (victorious army); Margaret (Pearl); Alice (truth).

The Puritans attached meanings to names: Mercy, Prudence, Patience, Faith, Hope, and Charity.

Names have meaning. If your name is *Charles*, you are strong and manly. If your name is *Donald*, you are a world ruler. If your name is *Click*, you talk incessantly!

God has a name. *God* means the supreme or ultimate reality. Why should the name of God be respected? It depends upon who you are. If you have little to do with God in the way of belief, the name of God can slip from your tongue without much thought of its meaning.

The Old Testament gives several names to describe God. For the Israelites, one name for God, "Yahweh," was so sacred they never spoke it aloud. They used an alternate word "Adonai." "Yahweh" means "I am that I am." That is to say that God has existed from the beginning and never ceases to exist. Yahweh or Jehovah describes God as being reliable, trustworthy, not fickle like the gods of other countries. Yahweh or Jehovah means that God is the same yesterday, today, and forever. The prophets came to realize that everything ultimately goes back to God. Nothing, they deciphered, can be independent of the power and purpose of God. Thus, they called God the *Eternal*. James Moffatt used that word in his translation of the Bible.

Other names given to God were *Elohim* — He is the vital power; *El Shaddai* — the Almighty God (Genesis 17:1). These names connote the attributes of God. Thus, a name has substance. Such a name as God commands respect.

Luther warned against the danger of misusing the name of God. There is the danger of thinking of God as remote. The other extreme is to think of God as so common that the deity is disrespected. Luther stated in the catechism that "we are to fear and love God so that we do not use his name to curse, swear, lie, or deceive, but call upon him in prayer, praise, and thanksgiving."

Our present age has diminished the sense of distance between God and human beings and made the concept of God commonplace. Whereas people may be a little lower than the angels, people today have the tendency to make God only a rung higher. He is, as one dentist described to me, "The tuxedo gentleman upstairs."

Street talk, shocking and realistic, has crept into television and movies. As a consequence, it is not surprising that God has been demeaned. Infiltrated by word associations, our culture tends to undermine decency and degrade the name of God. Four letter words, commonly used, indicate the meagerness of present-day vocabularies.

In his prayer, Jesus said, "Our Father ... hallowed be thy name." Luther in his answer to the first petition said, "The name of God is indeed holy in itself; but we pray in this petition that it may be hallowed also by us."

We can misuse God's name in flippant, careless talk. Once I played golf with three strangers, and it was not until the eighteenth hole that they learned I was a pastor. Apologies for their language came profusely. "You know," one fellow said, "our associations at work are of a pretty tough nature and this kind of talk becomes a habit. It doesn't mean anything," he said.

How clairvoyantly he spoke. People become victims of habit, and sin becomes a habit. If Christians cannot talk decently and honorably, who will call society to repentance? "It doesn't mean anything." When we say that, it means God is so little thought of that the tongue speaks without thought of God. God's name can be misused.

God's name can be abused, the greatest sin outwardly committed. This makes God lower than humankind. Is it not time to rethink the importance of this command?

There are right ways to use God's name. We are to call upon God, as the catechism states, "... in prayer, praise, and thanksgiving." The psalmist declares God's invitation: "Call on me in the day of trouble; I will deliver you, and you shall glorify me" (Psalm 50:15). The name of God is to be used in time of tribulation; it is to be used in worship; it is to be used in daily thanks to the Source of all good, the "Almighty God."

In the light of Christ, Old Testament conceptions of God take on a deeper meaning: righteousness, kindness, grace, long-suffering, compassion, and holiness. God's name is like that and requires respect.

The Third Commandment: "Remember the Sabbath day, to keep it holy."

"What does this mean for us? We are to fear and love God so that we do not neglect his Word and the preaching of it, but regard it as holy and gladly hear and learn it."

What is meant by the Sabbath day? It is derived from a Hebrew word translated to rest, to abstain from labor. For the Jew it was a sign of the covenant between God and his chosen people. Ezekiel 20:12 says, "Moreover I gave them my sabbaths, as a sign between me and them, so that they might know that I the Lord sanctify them." It was a day of rest in remembrance of what God had done at the time of creation.

The sabbath is strictly a Jewish derivative, although we know that many primitive races had "rest days." As Jewish history unfolded, the law of the sabbath became very strict. The Jew was careful to plan his work and his travels so that they did not conflict with the sacred day.

So strict was the law that they were shocked when Jesus healed on the sabbath. To the Jews the day had become a "no work" day and also a "no good works performed for God" day.

For many all that Sunday means is a day of rest, a day of a change of pace. Years ago the term "Christian Sabbath" was concocted to help Christians observe the Lord's Day. Despite efforts to destroy the idea that Sunday is the heir of the sabbath, Charlemagne (Frankish king, 742-814) made a decree in 789 which forbade all ordinary labor on Sunday a breach of this commandment.

Even today, some church members think of Sunday only as a day of rest and ask the question, "Why do we observe Sunday instead of Saturday?" forgetting that Saturday was an Old Testament practice.

Sunday is distinctly a Christian day. We should let it stand on its own merits. Christ rose from the dead on the first day of the week — Sunday. In observance of this, early Christians worshiped on Sunday. We do the same. We are to observe the Resurrection Day and keep it holy.

No one questions the need of a day or two off work a week. Primitive people saw the wisdom in that. People and beasts need rest and a change of pace. Bodily needs necessitate such a law.

But what some seem not to comprehend is that the mind and heart, as well as the body, need to keep a day holy. To keep one day in the week holy is to say that one day in the week we devote primarily to the hearing of God's Word.

Luther said: "... that on such a day of rest (since otherwise it cannot be accomplished) time and opportunity be taken to attend divine service, so that we meet to hear and treat of God's word, and afterward to praise God in singing and prayer."

He continued, "But this I say, is not so limited to any time, as with the Jews, that it must be just on this or that day; for in itself no one day is better than another, and this should indeed occur daily; but since the mass of people cannot give such attendance, there must be at least one day in the week that we set apart."

When a person says "Sunday is my only day off and I must rest," it is an indication that no Christian theology has pierced the soul. Such a person is saying in effect that God is not worth the time, the opposite connotation of the meaning of the word "worship."

The catechism states that we should not "... neglect his Word and the preaching of it, but regard it as holy and gladly hear and learn it." The question may well be asked: How could any Christian *neglect* it?

We can neglect it by indifference. We can neglect it by preoccupation with self interests. We can neglect it by overindulgence in recreation. Negligence translated means "there is no thought of God."

Churches abound in our country. If a Christian is away from home, he or she can usually find a church. If a Christian is out in the woods, a Bible in the hand is as important as a fishing rod, a ski on the foot, or a golf club.

Ah, how we have dismantled the effectiveness of this commandment! The Word is holy, God made a day in our busy schedules for worship so that we can "... gladly hear and learn it." From one worship celebration to the next, we should have grown in grace. The efficacy of this commandment is not in its resting but in its *reconciliation* with God. The Word gives us new understanding. That is pace change at its best.

Worship is natural for a believing heart. Candidly put: To refuse to worship is sin. Worship adds quality to life. Assurance of forgiveness and strength to live the Christian life come from worship.

God's name is holy and so is the day God has provided for people. Is there a connection between the two? Worship is the right use of God's name. Without worship how can people have pure thoughts? Without worship how can people regard their Maker with respect?

Respect is an act of giving particular attention to someone. Respect means having a high regard or esteem for someone. That Someone is God the Father, God the Son, and God the Holy Spirit.

Our culture could use a dash of respect. Comic Rodney Dangerfield is famous for protesting, "I don't get no respect." That's probably a good line for God, too. These two commandments command Christians to have respect for God. They build character.

III. Honor

The Fourth Commandment: "Honor your father and your mother."

"What does this mean for us? We are to fear and love God so that we do not despise or anger our parents and others in authority, but respect, obey, love, and serve them."

The Fifth Commandment: "You shall not kill."

"What does this mean for us? We are to fear and love God so that we do not hurt our neighbor in any way, but help him in all his physical needs."

From my rearview mirror I could see lights flashing off and on and in a few seconds a siren wailed. I quickly pulled off to the side of the road. "What's wrong?" said I to the officer who had slowly dismounted from his motorcycle and lumbered up to the open window of my car. "You were in the right lane and you must turn right when in that lane," said he with a half smile and a hidden burr in his voice. He calmly thrust a citation into my hand and gave me that half smile. Secretly in my heart, I questioned the existence of such a "right hand turn only" sign. Later, I swung the car around, re-tracked my original course, and there was the sign, big as life. I deserved the citation. The law was clear. Proceeding ahead without turning right endangered my life and possibly others. By breaking the law, I had taken my life into my own hands.

The ten commandments were placed by God alongside life's highway. Honoring God's signs is a way of trusting God. Disregarding the ten commandments endangers our own life and others.

Laws have existed since the beginning of civilization. Adam and Eve demonstrated humankind's tendency to ignore God's instructions about how to live in the garden, and were condemned to death.

Imagine Moses leading his people to the Promised Land over a span of forty years without laws! The Israelites would never have made it to the Holy Land without the ten commandments. We cannot come to Christian maturity without them, either.

This fourth commandment about honoring parents is about honoring family life. Family life for Moses and his people was different from ours. Children were disciplined by parents and learned to be obedient. They had good cause to do so. The Israelite father had complete ownership of his child, including the power of life and death. No wonder the commandment promises "... so that your days may be long and that it may go well with you in the land that the Lord your God is giving you" (Deuteronomy 5:16). It was dangerous to disobey a parent. Parents were in control. Blessing or curse from the parent meant everything to the child. Jacob wanted the blessing of his father, Isaac, so much that he cheated Esau, his brother, out of his birthright.

Twentieth-century family life was described in the 1950s as "The Revolt of the Children" (Elton Trueblood in *The Listener*, April 23, 1953). This label pointed to the greatest weakness prevalent in present-day family life — the breakdown of discipline. The breakdown of discipline involves loss of authority. Today, we are no longer shocked to hear of very young offenders who have engaged in violence and lawlessness. A perceptive observer remarked that they "do not always look brutish and savage, but they do look lonely, sullen, and proud."

In the last century and in this century, something has gone wrong at a deeper level. We build expensive homes and spend little time there. Activities of business, social life, school, and even church can draw the family apart. There is hardly a night free when all members are home at the same time. And, when a night is free, everybody gathers in the home theatre, the room darkened except for a single light bulb, where no intelligent conversation is carried on. Reading and discussion of meaningful family concerns are not priorities these days.

Elton and Pauline Trueblood in their book *The Recovery Of Family Life* warned us long ago that the "... trouble lies in philosophical confusion, especially about such great ideas as equality and freedom." They wrote, "Equality is often claimed by the young as their right, and interpreted as the notion that one person's opinion is as valuable as another's, even if the one is sixteen and ignorant, whereas the other is sixty and experienced." They said, "Personal respect is out of date. Many features in our current life, including educational tendencies of wide popularity, encourage the adolescent to suppose that he does not need to look up to anyone, and particularly not to his parents. The widespread loss of simple courtesy, which allows young people to be rude in criticism of their elders, may seem to some to be simply bad manners, but it may be in reality, a symptom of deep moral disorder" (pp. 104-105).

Add another dimension to this commandment. The fourth commandment for Moses and his people was primarily aimed at the adult. Because of their constant travels on the way to the Holy Land, the aged were abandoned when they could no longer work or walk, left to die by exposure or to be devoured by wildlife.

There is no doubt this commandment caused inconvenience for the Israelites. To care for the aged who could no longer care for themselves burdened the nation, with multiplying difficulties of food and shelter and conveyance. But the command brought into focus the reverence and care of life, the family ties that cannot be broken. Some who began the journey with Moses became the benefactors of God's law — the years had gone by and the older became aged.

Jesus' concern for his mother at Calvary is a fulfillment of this command. While in deathly pain, he thought about the welfare of his mother and assigned to the disciple John the responsibility of taking care of her. I find that not only commendable but insightful.

Medicine has honored this command. Death has been pushed back a few years. The "Advanced Youth," as the Chinese call it, now enjoy remarkable health in later years.

And, when health fails, institutions have been founded for the care of the aged. The church also has been interested in this command, and many Homes for the Aged are dotted across the land because of this interest. But, we must be careful about abandoning our aged to the care of society and the state. Every son or daughter is a son or daughter as long as one of his or her parents live. It is the duty of children to care for their parents in older age when they can no longer care for themselves.

But, why honor father and mother? In so doing, we honor God. The first three commandments specifically honor God. In these commandments, we honor the Creator's gift of human life. It is a matter of character.

When we come to the fifth commandment, "You shall not kill," another dimension in reverencing life is added.

Prince von Metternich (1773-1859, Austrian representative to France, statesman) once said to Napoleon Bonaparte concerning a military plan that was proposed, "That will cost 100,000 men." Napoleon replied, "What are the 100,000 men to me?" (*Catechetical Evangelization* by Baltzly, p. 83).

How cheap life seems to be. Newspapers and nightly newscasts seem to savor stories of homicide. Seldom can you see a movie without violence.

Moses assuredly had to deal with this problem again and again. God knows the brutality in the heart of people and that is why God said, "You shall not kill."

For the Israelites, it was not a sin to delegate to proper authorities the execution of offenders. They did not forbid the slaying of animals. They believed in capital punishment. They killed enemies in times of war. For them, the commandment was given to protect human life within the community of Israel, protecting one Israelite from another.

There are many ways of breaking this commandment. Luther said we are not to "... hurt our neighbor in any way, but help him in all his physical needs." Alexander Maclaren, in his *Expositions Of Holy Scripture*, added "A man who looks on while another drowns, or who sends a ship out half-manned and overloaded, breaks it as readily as a red-handed murderer."

Jesus carried it further: "You have heard that it was said to those of ancient times, 'You shall not murder'; and 'whoever murders shall be liable to judgment.' But I say to you that if you are angry with a brother or sister, you will be liable to judgment; and if you insult a brother or sister, you will be liable to the council; and if you say, 'You fool,' you will be liable to the hell of fire" (Matthew 5:21-22).

Why did Jesus say that? God looks on the heart. The wish, in God's sight, is as serious as the deed. Many a murder would have been committed if it had not been for fear of the consequences. Hidden desires lead to open deeds. Hatred, selfishness, pride — all are enemies to the soul.

Ella Wheeler Wilcox (1855-1919), American poet and journalist, wrote a disturbing poem, "The Revealing Angels," which I have never been able to get out of my mind. In it she describes the vilest sinners of earth:

Suddenly and without warning they came,
The Revealing Angels came.
Suddenly and simultaneously, through city streets.
Through quiet lanes and country roads they walked;
They walked, crying, "God has sent us to find
The vilest sinners of earth.
We are to bring them before Him, before the Lord of
   Life."

Their voices were like bugles;
And then all war, all strife,
And all the noises of the world grew still;
And no one talked;
And no one toiled, but many strove to flee away.
Robbers and thieves, and those sunk in drunkenness
   and crime,
Men and women of evil repute,
And mothers with fatherless children in their arms, all
   strove to hide.
But the Revealing Angels passed them by,
Saying: "Not you, not you.
Another day, when we shall come again
Unto the haunts of men,
Then we shall call your names;
But God has asked us first to bring to Him
Those guilty of greater shames

Than lust, or theft, or drunkenness, or vice,
Yea, greater than murder done in passion,
Or self-destruction done in dark despair.
Now in His Holy Name we call 'Come one and all;
Come forth; reveal your faces.' "

Then through the awful silence of the world,
Where noise had ceased, they came,
The sinful hosts.
They came from lowly and from lofty places,
Some poorly clad, but many clothed like queens;
They came from scenes of revel and from toil,
From haunts of sin, from palaces, from homes,
From boudoirs, and from churches.
They came like ghosts —
The vast brigades of women who had slain
Their helpless, unborn children. With them trailed
Lovers and husbands who had said, "Do this."
And those who helped for hire.
They stood before the Angels, before the Revealing
 Angels they stood
And they heard the Angels say
And all the listening world heard the Angels say: "These
 are the
Vilest sinners of all...."

Whether you share the poet's belief or not, and whether or not you sanction Supreme Court edicts and certain laws of the land that make abortion legal, all the sins enumerated in that poem can be forgiven. "... Though your sins are like scarlet, they shall be like snow; though they are red like crimson, they shall become like wool" (Isaiah 1:18).

"The Revealing Angels," however, did not ferret out the vilest sin of all. The vilest sin of all is *unbelief.* God does not choose to forgive the sin of unbelief.

In both the fourth and fifth commandments, there is the call of God to parents and children to honor one another, and for everybody to honor life. The bottom line is: Have you broken any commandments? And if so, have you called upon God to forgive you? Do you feel God's cleansing up and down your spine?

We are to call upon God to guide us along life's highway, well marked by the ten commandments. Honoring the commandments puts us in God's hands. They help build character.

IV. Chastity And Fairness

The Sixth Commandment: "You shall not commit adultery."

"What does this mean for us? We are to fear and love God so that in matters of sex our words and conduct are pure and honorable, and husband and wife love and respect each other."

The Seventh Commandment: "You shall not steal."

"What does this mean for us? We are to fear and love God so that we do not take our neighbor's money or property, or get them in any dishonest way, but help our neighbor to improve and protect his property and means of making a living."

Sin has a way of strangling the sinner. Suppose your sins are just little ones: a glance at a woman or man with a gleam in the eye without thought of letting it go further; a reporting of a few more dollars in the *charitable contribution* column on the income tax report than actually given.

Sins grow up. They are dangerous. A father in Pennsylvania out cutting wood found a little black bear cub, only a week old. The bear was so beautiful he took it home. His little daughter loved the cub, fed it with a spoon, and played with it. The bear became the family pet, was exceedingly playful, and was allowed to roam about the house as well as out of doors. It grew rapidly and was as playful as ever. When the bear was a year old, some friends admonished the little girl that she should be careful lest the bear hurt her. Putting her arms around the bear and hugging him up close, she said, "You won't hurt me, will you, Bruno?" The bear stuck his bed red tongue out and looked at her as if to say, "Of course, I wouldn't hurt you." Six months later the little girl was playing with Bruno and the bear struck her a blow with his paw which killed her. The fact that the bear had been brought up with the family did not change the disposition of the bear. He had just become a bear with a big bear's nature.

The disposition of sin, by its very nature, is to kill. Paul put it this way: "For the wages of sin is death" (Romans 6:23).

The sixth commandment states: "You shall not commit adultery." Do you suppose the breaking of any of the other commandments has done as much harm? Hearts broken; careers ruined; tragedies caused; suffering inflicted; children cheated; deaths resulted. What a big bear this animal "adultery."

In Moses' time marriage was an institution. Most everyone was married. The problem was adultery, the dishonoring of marriage. This commandment helped protect the husband's property rights in his wife or concubine. It helped to guarantee the legitimacy of his offspring.

The commandment also made Jewish society different from pagan societies. It was the first step in true reverence of women.

It called for a control of passion. It called for a reverence for marriage. It warned against dictatorship of the body.

In Luther's time, adultery was a problem also. He said, "What you must say is: Even though I do have chances to kick over the traces, nevertheless, since God says, 'Fear me!' I will not do it. Even though the emperor will not find it out, God who is above me will. Therefore say, O my God, grant me grace that I may not fall and that I may keep my marriage pure. This means you are to live chastely in your marriage, in body, words, gestures, and heart. That's why God gave to each his wife" (*Luther's Works, op. cit.*, p. 154).

There is much more to the sixth commandment in Deuteronomy, chapters 22-25, for the purity of Israel's life pertained not only to marital life but to single life. The Israelites were tough on people who misused sex. The offender was often put to death. If a girl was discovered not to be a virgin at the time of marriage, the groom could take her back to the entrance of her father's house and men of the town would stone her to death. On the other hand, if the groom trumped up the story, he could be fined 100 silver shekels and could not divorce her.

It is evident that Israel had some laws which do not pertain to today: for example, levirate marriage, wherein a brother has to become husband to a deceased brother's widow, and the practice of noted leaders having concubines. It is to be noted, however, that their intent was to preserve the human family. The bottom line in these scriptures is that promiscuity is a sin. Sex is one of God's greatest gifts, but to misuse sex is sin.

Sexual promiscuity is wrong for five good reasons:
1. Promiscuity dishonors God's intent for human life.
2. Promiscuity dishonors self.
3. Promiscuity dishonors one's body.
4. Promiscuity impoverishes personality.
5. Promiscuity is dangerous, with possible disease leading to death.

These reasons alone tell us that misuse of sex is sin.

Furthermore, I wonder what Luther would have thought about the bodily gyrations begun by Elvis Presley? I wonder what Luther's reaction would be if he attended one of Hollywood's Oscar events, with women baring their breasts or slitting their dresses down to their buttocks, casting their pearls among swine? Or, young "ladies" bearing their breasts before thousands at a sports event? I wonder what he would have said about parked cars in the dark — young people's experiments and exploration of the human heart and body? I wonder what he would have thought about people living together without commitment to marriage? I wonder what he would have thought about our language which at times appears only able to describe feelings with four-letter words? I wonder what he would have thought about our sex movies or pornography on the Internet? He might get the idea that all we think about and talk about is sex.

I rather think Luther would let Jesus say it: "You have heard that it was said, 'You shall not commit adultery.' But I say to you that everyone who looks at a woman with lust has already committed adultery with her in his heart" (Matthew 5:27-28).

Sodom and Gomorrah sex acts are gaining ground in this present age and the church seems uncertain about what to make of all this. Scripture quoting doesn't seem to settle it, and we are a long way from healing in matters of sex.

Meanwhile, the bottom line for us is to keep chaste in matters of sex. Present-day society has gone to extremes and is alienating itself from God. The Christian is to love and honor God, and to use his or her body in a dignified and pure way. That's exactly what the word *chaste* means. *Webster's Dictionary* defines chaste as "pure in thought and act." Isn't that what God expects of Christians?

Little sins have a way of growing up. They are indications of a deeper cancer — alienation from God. Your body is a temple meant for God to live in. Your eye is a part of that temple; your mind is a part of that temple; your arms and legs are a part of that temple; your private parts are a part of that temple.

Saint Paul stated, "... Do you not know that your body is a temple of the Holy Spirit within you, which you have from God, and that you are not your own? For you were bought with a price; therefore glorify God in your body" (1 Corinthians 6:19-20).

The commandment, "You shall not steal," is equally important. Property, as well as person, must be secured. Stealing is taking or keeping what is not ours. It is also loss of property caused by carelessness, fraudulent dealings in business, and poor stewardship. It is a matter of fairness.

How do you feel when this commandment speaks to your conscience?

What the catechism says is true: "It is the smallest part of the thieves that are hung. If we are to hang them all, where shall we get rope enough?" Someone said if a prosperous gentleman should pray, "Incline our hearts to keep this law," and his prayer was answered, he would have to live more modestly!

These commandments condemn us all. If a child spends his or her lunch money for a treat instead, that is stealing. If a person takes advantage of a client, that is stealing. If a church member leaves God last or not at all on the list for distribution of his or her funds, that is stealing. God is robbed. It is a matter of fairness.

The Israelite world was out of joint, too. Some people had everything the heart could desire. Millions had little. That's why politicians pretend to wrestle with it every election time. I wish they would come right out and say it is about fairness. We could use a dash of fairness in this country.

The right to possess is clearly inferred in this commandment. But people need to understand that they are only possessors, not owners. A steward of God, therefore, must give an account to God of his or her administration of God's possessions. Humankind needs to recognize that his or her neighbor was created by God also. People are to help their neighbor, including assisting the neighbor to find a job and giving fair consideration to the neighbor's needs. Every person has a place in this world. Every person is a part of God's purpose. A helping hand, a healing heart, and a mind mindful of others could help this old world realize God is the sole owner.

Little sins of lustful eyes, of snatching time from employers, or of cheating on an exam, have a way of growing up. People can live in the false hope that their sins will be forever secret.

Edgar Allen Poe's striking story, "The Black Cat," tells of this. In a certain family there was a black cat. The husband hated the cat and the cat knew it. One day he threw a blackjack at the cat and put out one of its eyes. This made the cat more fearful and watchful. The husband hated his wife, too. One day he killed her and hid her body in a section of the cellar wall, rebuilding the wall so well that he left no evidence of it having been torn down. He then reported the disappearance of his wife.

Knowing the disposition of the man, the police made an inspection of the house. With boldness the man bade them look everywhere, tapping the walls with his cane, bidding them to make sure nothing was hid. As he tapped on the wall, they heard the mewing of a cat behind the wall. In fear the cat had hidden itself. The police tore down the wall and in turn found the body of the wife.

You can commit adultery or be promiscuous or steal in secret. The Bible says, however, "... be sure your sin will find you out" (Numbers 32:23).

Sin, like a bear, is by nature destructive; like a cat it cannot be hidden. Size of sins makes no difference. They all cry out in defiance of God. Sin pays off in spiritual death.

Keeping these commandments will cause life to fall into place, as God intended. You just can't beat chastity and fairness. Chastity and fairness make life livable. Dishonorable sex and cheating always fail. Love never fails. It is a matter of character.

V. Truthfulness

The Eighth Commandment: "You shall not bear false witness against your neighbor."

"What does this mean for us? We are to fear and love God so that we do not betray, slander, or lie about our neighbor, but defend him, speak well of him, and explain his actions in the kindest way."

While in Argentina directing evangelism missions, I preached in a church in Buenos Aires. It was August, in the middle of winter for them. There was no heat in the church building. I wore a topcoat underneath my robe. I looked like a football player!

After worship I was invited to a home for Sunday dinner. The pastor alerted me that the family had gone to considerable expense in providing the dinner. I took that to mean that I was in for an Argentine treat.

My hostess served a meal in elegant Argentinian style. The main dish was lamb's tongue. When I was a boy on the farm I had a pet lamb. Because of this, I never ate lamb. Furthermore, the tongue of an animal is not too delectable, in my opinion, although some people crave it, especially the Argentinians.

There set before me was something I literally detest — lamb's tongue. Placing the most charitable construction upon my host and hostess, I realized this meal was meant to honor me, for lamb's tongue to the Argentinian was a delicacy and costly.

It was difficult to smile or carry on a conversation while eating that lamb's tongue. I did well and should have received an academy award for my performance. In fact, I did so well that while my head was turned my hostess, without asking me, placed a second helping before me. On that day I nearly died — I ate two lambs' tongues!

The human tongue must be much harder for God to swallow. In the Garden of Eden the first lie was told. The serpent spoke to

Eve: "You will not die, for God knows that when you eat of it your eyes will be opened, and you will be like God, knowing good and evil" (Genesis 3:4-5). This is why Luther called Satan the "father of lies."

When Adam and Eve heard God walking in the garden in the cool of the day, they hid. God said, " 'Who told you that you were naked? Have you eaten from the tree of which I commanded you not to eat?' The man said, 'The woman whom you gave to be with me, she gave me fruit from the tree, and I ate.' Then the Lord God said to the woman, 'What is this you have done?' The woman said, 'The serpent tricked me, and I ate.' ... The Lord God said ... and to dust you shall return" (Genesis 3:11-14, 19).

It was a tongue that originated sin. It was a tongue that caused human eyes to see nakedness, to comprehend good and evil. It was a human tongue which said in reply to God's query about the whereabouts of Cain's brother, "I do not know; am I my brother's keeper?" (Genesis 4:9). It was a human tongue which answered Isaac, "Are you really my son Esau?" Jacob replied, "I am" (Genesis 27:24). It was a human tongue which denied Jesus Christ at a central point in history. "You also were with Jesus the Galilean." Peter lied, "I do not know the man!" (Matthew 26:69, 74). Humankind's tongue has been hard for God to swallow.

Lying is also hard for people to swallow. What home can exist on lies? Some thoughtless persons coupled the names of a young widow and a young married man. The man's wife went out of her mind in jealousy. In anguish, she took the law into her own hands and shot to death her husband. Then she ruthlessly and cruelly killed the young widow. Later it turned out she was mistaken. She had taken gossip at face value. But, it was too late. Three lives were destroyed. Those who spread the story were just as guilty. Married life must be built on truth, not lies.

Children must have confidence in their parents. What child can trust a lying father or mother? If a child asks a question, it should be honored and answered right away in language understandable to the child. Parents are tempted not to take time to use their tongues to help channel a child's imagination.

There are parents who threaten their children with dire consequences unless they do not do something, and then frequently relent when disobedience persists. If you promise a child discipline for disobedience, fulfill it even though it's difficult. A child's life must be built on truth, not lies.

False witness in society is hard to swallow. A cashier resigned from a bank. Shortly after he retired from his position, which he had honorably and faithfully served for many years, someone started a story that he guessed Mr. Smith was asked to retire. Someone added that he presumed there were some discrepancies in his accounts.

In a little while, the whole town was wagging its tongue about Mr. Smith's dishonesty. "Who would have thought he was that sort?" they said. People shunned him. His old friends had little to do with him. Finally, Mr. Smith asked one of his close associates what was the reason for this distant attitude on the part of people. When he was told, he was so astonished and overcome that he dropped dead.

False witness in business is hard to swallow. Television commercials can claim too much for a product. There are often "come-ons," cleverly stated advertisements to entice an individual to the scene of business in order to sell him or her something more expensive. "You really don't want this," the salesperson will explain in referring to the item advertised. "It is inferior material."

False witness in politics is standard procedure, especially during elections. The person we might think is honest and decent may be shredded to pieces, lie by lie. Shakespeare's Othello (Act III, Scene 3) spoke the truth:

He who steals my purse steals trash;
But he who filches from me my good name
Robs me of that which not enriches him
and makes me poor indeed.

False witness in religion is hard to swallow. Dr. Baltzly, in his catechetical book, writes, "Those institutions like Christian Science and the Unitarian Church are guilty of religious lies, for they pretend to be churches in which men and women shall find salvation, when in fact they deny the deity of our Lord Jesus Christ, belief in which is essential to salvation. Like priests and prophets in the Old Testament, they are saying to their members, 'Peace, peace,' when there is no peace" (*Catechetical Evangelization*, p. 119).

There are many religions in our day which deny the divinity of Christ. They are the greatest liars of all. We must protect people from them by being true witnesses to the Christ.

The tongue can be a wonderful instrument for God. "All of them were filled with the Holy Spirit and began to speak in other languages (tongues), as the Spirit gave them ability" (Acts 2:4). The disciples witnessed in several languages.

Most people we associate with understand and speak English. Can we not witness in one language? As in the opening words of Matins, "O Lord, open my lips, and my mouth shall declare your praise" (*Lutheran Book of Worship*, p. 131). That's all we need to ask of God. And that is all God asks of us, "... for we cannot keep from speaking about what we have seen and heard" (Acts 4:20).

There are many ways to break this commandment, "You shall not bear false witness against your neighbor." There are social lies, professional lies, half-truths, lying by inaccuracies, white lies, living a lie, and lying by inference.

All lies are detected and detested by God. "Do not be deceived; God is not mocked, for you reap whatever you sow" (Galatians 6:7).

Life hinges upon honesty. We either believe Jesus when he said, "The Father and I are one" (John 10:30), or we believe the lies of people who reduce Christ to a mere teacher.

The Christian is admonished by Christ, "In everything do to others, as you would have them do to you; for this is the law and the prophets" (Matthew 7:12). Luther put it in his catechism, "We are to fear and love God so that we do not betray, slander, or lie about our neighbor, but defend him, speak well of him, and explain his actions in the kindest way."

In so doing, we keep high standards, set by God ages ago. We build up the habit of making discriminating and constructive comments about people. This is God's will. Truthfulness is God's way.

I did not like the lamb's tongue set before me. How does God like your tongue? Have you thought well, whenever possible, of the people you know? Have you spoken well of them, picking out their good rather than their bad qualities? Have you made a conscious effort to further the good qualities in them? Have you spoken to others about the resurrected Jesus Christ? Have you led someone to Christ?

In answering these questions, we are led to a repentant attitude, a desire for God's forgiveness, and a determination, by the Holy Spirit, to live in accordance with God's will. Truthfulness is the best way to honor God and others. It is a demonstration of character.

VI. Neighborliness

The Ninth Commandment: "You shall not covet your neighbor's house."

"What does this mean for us? We are to fear and love God so that we do not desire to get our neighbor's possessions by scheming, or by pretending to have a right to them, but always help him keep what is his."

The Tenth Commandment: "You shall not covet your neighbor's wife, or his manservant, or his maidservant, or his cattle, or anything that is your neighbor's."

"What does this mean for us? We are to fear and love God so that we do not tempt or coax away from our neighbor his wife or his workers, but encourage them to remain loyal."

Did you ever have a neighbor who vexed your spirit? I had such a neighbor. My neighbor and I seesawed on these commandments of not coveting over a period of several months. It was not a verbal exchange. It bordered on the ridiculous. Like a silent screen picture, the words were only dubbed into our minds without any audible sounding off.

It all started with a property marker. Since our house was new, the surveyor of our property planted into the ground markers on each corner of the lot. Properly recorded in city hall, along with a description of the land and the location of the house, I felt certain our property rights were clear and could not be questioned.

But, my neighbor evidently could not believe one corner marker was correct. Early in the morning and late at night, he and his wife would squint at that marker and walk around it. Finally, they decided to move the marker. They drove an iron post into the ground leaving it about two feet above ground, at a place they felt the marker should go, much to their benefit of course! Now, what should I do? Should I confront them? Should I move the peg?

I didn't do either. All I did was pound the post level with the ground so that the children would not fall on it and be seriously hurt. Later, the neighbor and his wife came along, pulled the peg up, repounded it in a new place giving them even more ground, still leaving the post dangerously high off the ground. I gave up and stacked a woodpile next to his post and the issue was settled!

God has given us certain property rights. They are recorded in Exodus and Deuteronomy — the ten commandments. Because we have been given free will, we can move one of God's commands or markers to satisfy personal desires. That is what God calls coveting. Coveting is setting aside or moving God's marker.

A young lady wanted to make friends happy at Christmas. She bought them presents and charged everything. Because her employer had high regard for her and because she made a good salary, firms from which she purchased these presents permitted her to charge the Christmas gifts.

After Christmas the bills began to come in. She became overwhelmed with debt. As the firms began to press for payment, she became panicky. One day when she had the deposit book of her employer ready for the bank, she went into the closet to get her coat and hat, and returning to her desk cried out, "Did that man come in who opened the door a moment ago?" Her employer asked why. She said, "Someone has robbed the deposit book," and began to shed tears. Her employer consoled her while she upbraided herself for having left the book on the desk. Her gracious employer exonerated her from blame and asked her to check how much was missing. She soon reported $75. Afterward, she took the checks to the bank and cashed them.

Weeks later the employer was looking over his cancelled checks and discovered a check for $200 unaccounted for. After investigation, he realized his secretary had forged his name.

The incident shows how desire can run away with a person and lead one into an unlawful deed.

You can desire an automobile, but if you steal an automobile, you have moved one of God's markers. You can desire to go to the beach, but if you neglect duty, it is wrong. You can desire to have money, but the desire that moves a person to cheat or steal or defraud in order to get the money moves God's marker. The desire to be wealthy can be a rightful goal, but to take undue advantage of another person in order to reach your goal disregards the rights of another. It moves God's marker. The desire to get good grades in school is commendable, but if you cheat in order to get them, you have moved God's marker. The desire to have your own wife or husband is natural, but the desire to have someone else's wife or husband is wrong.

Right desire is good and necessary. Paul said so in 1 Corinthians 12:31, "... Strive for the greater gifts...." But, desire which runs loose, disregarding God and the property rights of others is all wrong. This is coveting.

Moving God's marker means letting desire deceive. When Naaman, the successful Syrian commander-in-chief of the army of King Aram, went to Elisha, Israel's prophet, to be healed of his leprosy and was cured, he offered Elisha many personal gifts. Elisha refused and simply and humbly said, "Go in peace" (2 Kings 5:19). Gehazi, the servant of Elisha, desired those gifts. After Naaman left, Gehazi followed and stopped Naaman down the road and said to him, "My master has sent me to say, 'Two members of a company of prophets have just come to me from the hill country of Ephraim; please give them a talent of silver and two changes of clothing.' " Naaman gave Gehazi not only two changes of garments but two talents of silver. Gehazi kept them for himself. When queried by Elisha, Gehazi denied the deceit, but Elisha knew better. He said, " '... The leprosy of Naaman shall cling to you, and your descendents forever.' So he left his presence leprous, as white as snow" (2 Kings 5:27).

Gehazi had moved God's marker. Silver and clothing were his desire. They did not last. Leprosy did.

It was desire that caused David to arrange for the death of Bathsheba's husband, Uriah. David thought only of pleasure when he sent for Uriah's wife. David thought he could cover up his crime. Nathan, the prophet, confronted him by telling him a story about a rich man who had many flocks and herds. This rich man, Nathan asserted, took the one little ewe lamb of a poor man to feed a traveler. David swallowed the story hook, line, and sinker, and said the rich man should be punished. Nathan looked him in the eye and said, "You are the man!" (2 Samuel 12:7). David's sin brought him wretchedness.

It was desire that caused Judas to take the thirty pieces of silver in exchange for the betrayal of our Lord. In despair, Judas hung himself.

Covetousness brings nothing but misery. It likes to paint everything as beautiful, charming, desirable, pleasant. It doesn't respect family relationships, as when Jacob tricked Esau into selling his birthright and tricked his blind parent into believing he was his brother Esau (Genesis 27). It respects nothing and nobody. It is the master of the soul which permits the moving of God's marker.

God's marker is meant to be buried deep in your heart. Jesus said, "Take care! Be on guard against all kinds of greed, for one's life does not consist in the abundance of possessions" (Luke 12:15).

This is Jesus' way of telling us that our happiness does not consist in the gratification of improper desires. These commandments teach us that happiness is not to be found in the things of this world. Jesus emphasized it; he illustrated it by his life. At the cross, his only possession was a robe.

Human nature can trick us. Seldom do we rejoice in the successes of others. We are jealous and suspicious creatures. We endeavor to acquire as much wealth as we can without much regard for others. We pretend to be godly and as Luther exclaimed "conceal our rascality." We camouflage all this by calling it "shrewdness" and "caution." The teacher who had two wives eight miles apart lived a double life for a while but his covetousness caught up with him.

No one is free from guilt. Like the other commandments, we are constantly accused, as they show us how ungodly we are in the sight of God. Although civil law may let us go free, God does not. God sees the deceitful heart as well as the malice prevalent in the world.

Luther, in the *Large Catechism*, states, "... We abide by the common senses of these commandments, that in the first place we do not desire our neighbor harm, nor even assist nor give occasion for it, but gladly leave and see him in the enjoyment of his own, besides advance and preserve for him what may be for his profit and service, as we should wish to be treated. Thus these commandments are especially given against envy and miserable avarice, that God may remove all causes and sources whence arises everything by which we do injury to our neighbor, and therefore he expresses it in plain words: Thou shall not covet, etc." (p. 434).

The non-Christian does not see the Great Surveyor of Life and his markers. Paul said, "Do you not know that wrongdoers will not inherit the kingdom of God? Do not be deceived! Fornicators, idolaters, adulterers, male prostitutes, sodomites, thieves, the greedy, drunkards, revilers, robbers — none of these will inherit the kingdom of God" (1 Corinthians 6:9-10).

The Christian ponders these things in the heart. In fact, bury them deep. Let no neighbor change them. Let not circumstance nor emotion cloud your vision and deceive you. Love the Lord God with all your heart. As Paul said in Romans 10:10, "For one believes with the heart and so is justified, and one confesses with the mouth and so is saved." And again in Romans 10:5-9, "Moses writes concerning the righteousness that comes from the law, that 'the person who does these things will live by them.' But the righteousness that comes from faith says ... The word is near you, on your lips and in your heart ... because if you confess with your lips that Jesus is Lord and believe in your heart that God raised him from the dead, you will be saved." God's markers are not always discerned. Actually, they are simply written in the heart in the form of a cross.

Luther finalizes the commandments with a question: "What does God say of all these commandments? He says: 'I, the Lord your God, am a jealous God, visiting the iniquity of the fathers upon the children to the third and fourth generation of those who hate me, but showing steadfast love to thousands of those who love me and keep my commandments.' " Then Luther concludes with the familiar question: "What does this mean for us? God warns that he will punish all who break these commandments. Therefore we are to fear his wrath and not disobey him. But he promises grace and every blessing to all who keep these commandments. Therefore we are to love and trust him, and gladly do what he commands."

Thus, we have the ten commandments, laws of the land, character builders, a compend of doctrine. The Eiffel Tower in Paris, France, which we spoke of in the first chapter, stands as one of the greatest engineering feats of all time. From the top platform the view can be seen for 85 miles.

Look down at the base of the commandments, "I am the Lord your God ..." See its columns rising into the sky with reverence for God's name and day, with respect for parents and elders, marriage and home, with cleanness of mouth, with rightful acknowledgment of the properties of others.

On the top platform, conscious of the base and columns, we look out to the grand view of life. How wonderful God has made it. He has given us land and loved ones. He has showered us with thought and thankfulness. And, in the distance, there is a cross. See it? And still farther ahead — an empty grave! See it? What a life, now and to come, with relatives and friends safely in the arms of Jesus. What a God we have! He is the basis of all. In heaven there will be no land markers. Everything will be ours for we are God's! It's a matter of character.

Part Two: Declarations

VII. Kingdom People

"Blessed are the poor in spirit, for theirs is the kingdom of heaven" (Matthew 5:3).

Years ago when Richard Shepard, pastor of St. Martin's Church in downtown London, died, the congregation lost a great pastor. It was said he had restored life and joy in the congregation. A newspaper showed a picture of the pulpit of that church. The Bible was lying open. Underneath the picture were these words: "Here endeth the first lesson."

That's the way the beatitudes of Our Lord strike me. They are the first lesson in Christian living. It would have been better if they had nailed such words atop the cross of Christ instead of labeling him "King of the Jews." Jesus is king in the art of spelling out in short sentences the summary of Christian character. They are the introduction to the greatest sermon ever preached, recorded in the fifth, sixth, and seventh chapters of Matthew.

These words were spoken from a sitting position. While in seminary one of our students was severely injured in an automobile accident, thereafter confined to a wheelchair. We took turns carrying him around, as necessity demanded. There were no ramps for wheelchairs in those days! He preached from a wheelchair. From that sitting position he commanded attention and respect. His "senior sermon," as we were required to do, preached before fellow students and faculty, was a highlight of my seminary days.

Jesus preached or taught — both have the same impact — from a sitting position. It wasn't because he could not stand. He was following a rabbinical custom. When a rabbi spoke from a sitting position, he was speaking as an authentic spokesperson for God. The professor's "chair" is derived from this background.

Matthew wrote about this event in Jesus' ministry in descriptive detail. When he says Jesus "... began to speak," his point is this: Jesus spoke with courage. He did not shrink from what needed to be said. In the Psalms we read of the "poor," the characterization of the true people of God, "... those who know their lives are not in their own control and that they are dependent on God. 'Poor in spirit' makes this explicit" (*The New Interpreter's Bible, Volume VIII*, p. 178, by M. Eugene Boring).

For many years I gave Jesus' Sermon on the Mount from memory as the sermon of the day. It usually takes 22 minutes to preach. I can testify to the fact that hearers squirm when they hear Jesus' words articulated. For example, when Jesus said, "Why do you see the speck in your neighbor's eye, but do not notice the log in your own eye? Or how can you say to your neighbor, 'Let me take the speck out of your eye, while the log is in your own eye?' You hypocrite, first take the log out of your own eye, and then you will see clearly to take the speck out of your neighbor's eye" (Matthew 7:3-5).

Any preacher using the language Jesus used might not be crucified but could be criticized, if not chastised! I remember a lady in my first parish saying to me, "I didn't like it when you looked right at me and raised your right eyebrow." (I probably did raise an eyebrow!)

The first lesson in the declarative beatitudes is, "Blessed are the poor in spirit, for theirs is the kingdom of heaven."

Consider Jesus' use of the word "poor." What's so blessed about being poor? When I learned a friend inherited three million dollars I was envious, especially since he was already a millionaire. I could hear myself talking to myself about how I would like to have a little slice of his inheritance. I wouldn't have to worry about making ends meet every month. And, many of you could ask the same question: What's so "blessed" about being poor?

A service station attendant told me, after he asked me what I did for a living (I didn't have my clerical collar on and told him I wrote a few books), that he had written a book about his experiences as a vagrant for two years. He deliberately became a homeless person in order to experience what it means to be destitute. One of his comments stuck in my memory. He said, "I had the feeling of having no power, no prestige, and no influence." He said he was insulted as well as assaulted. He now knows what it means to be poor.

In this society of the new millennium, most do not know what it means to be poor. I do. I was around when the stock market crashed in 1929 and as a teenager experienced the difficulties of a nationwide depression. The "bread lines" still stick in my memory.

Thousands of people staged daily demonstrations in The Poor People's Campaign of 1968, in Washington, D.C. Affluent America did not think highly of the idea of building a "shantytown" within the shadow of the Capitol. And, when the rains came with its mud, and the accompanying problems of sanitation and health, and all the other problems connected with keeping thousands of poor people in the heart of one of our great cities, many rejoiced when Shantytown, U.S.A., had to be abandoned. Some applauded when the bulldozers came into view, clearing away the debris, once more making our nation's capital beautiful and safe for democracy.

The feelings were so intense about The Poor People's Campaign that one of my fellow pastors who housed some of the poor in the church building, without the approval of a congregational meeting, had to leave that parish and eventually left the ministry.

The mistake that those in charge of The Poor People's Campaign made was not stating over and over again that the unfortunate circumstances which occurred in Washington due to the elements were some of the very conditions which make poor people poor. Without opportunity, without funds, the poor cannot fight the elements, cannot fight circumstances, and cannot experience being a full member of society. The countless homeless in this country is a present-day case in point — people with "no power, no prestige, and no influence." Even good people in a parish I served had difficulty reconciling the use of their exterior sign as a shield and sleeping place for a homeless person. Most of us have no concept of what it means to be poor.

Jesus would not have been oblivious to The Poor People's Campaign, if he had made a personal appearance at that time. He was not oblivious to the tyranny of Rome and the bigotry of Jerusalem. I don't think Jesus would be oblivious to the problems of the homeless, the hopeless, and the hungry. That's why he labeled so-called "religious people" in his day hypocrites. He said, "For I tell you, unless your righteousness exceeds that of the scribes and Pharisees, you will never enter the kingdom of heaven." Today he might say, "For I tell you, unless your righteousness exceeds that of American culture, you will never enter the kingdom of heaven."

Jesus used the word "poor" deliberately. He knew what it means to be poor. Born in a stable, crucified on a city dump, with a seamless robe the only legacy left for his persecutors, he was poor. This is what makes the beatitude "Blessed are the poor in spirit ..." believable. Jesus took what the world considers paramount, earthly savings, and proved it to be folly "... where moth and rust consume and where thieves break in and steal...." He beckons us to share with the least of humankind, "Truly I tell you, just as you did it to one of the least of these who are members of my family, you did it to me" (Matthew 25:40). Kingdom people share.

We cannot understand this beatitude unless we know something of what it means to be poor "with no power, no prestige, and no influence."

The beatitude tells us there is a difference between happiness and bliss. The word "happiness" has its root meaning "hap" which means "chance." Happiness, therefore, depends upon chance and/or the circumstances of life. That is why so many people looking for happiness never find it. They are looking for happiness in things or circumstances. If you seek happiness, you are no better than the nonbeliever. The "Don't worry; be happy" craze was a shallow philosophy.

The word "blessed" means something else. It means "bliss." Whereas happiness is more subjective, bliss is more objective. It is a look at God. The reason why the disciples were called blessed was because they possessed the qualities which made them receptive to God's gifts.

For example, it is impossible to help an alcoholic if an alcoholic insists he or she is not one. The first lesson an alcoholic has to learn is to accept the fact of being an alcoholic. This is hard to do. It involves confession. It involves swallowing one's pride. It involves the acknowledgment that a person needs help.

Good people are much like the alcoholic. It is hard for "good" people to learn the first lesson — that they are ill without God, that they are incomplete without God, that they are helpless, and that they need someone beyond themselves.

You have "bliss" or you are "blessed" when you embrace helplessness. You and I are powerless without God. Blessed is the person who learns that he or she is destitute without God. When you and I declare our dependence upon God, we become independent of everything else. With God, the impossible becomes possible. Regardless of what happens to us, in spite of everything, we can maintain integrity. With God, we re-evaluate our lives. We are blessed when we do that. Without God, we are poor regardless of how rich we are. With God, we are rich regardless of how poor we are. This is a description and a declaration of character.

The disciples were blessed because they had the qualities which made them receptive to God's gifts. They admitted they were helpless without Christ. "Lord, to whom can we go? You have the words of eternal life," answered Peter when Jesus asked the disciples if they, too, like the crowd, wanted to go away because of the difficulty of accepting his words (John 6:68). So, they re-evaluated the meaning of true wealth and were willing to leave all and follow him. They discovered independence through their dependence upon God. They became independent of the changes and chances in life when they walked out of the Upper Room following the resurrection, no more afraid of what would happen to them, intent upon telling others of their dependence upon God.

The world cannot give a faith like that. It cannot take away a faith like that. That is why Jesus said to them, "Blessed are the poor in spirit, for theirs is the kingdom of heaven." Kingdom is where God rules. When God rules the human heart, heaven begins and continues to eternity. A person becomes a kingdom person.

Oh, the bliss of the person who realizes that. Oh, the bliss of a person who accepts the will of God for life. Oh, the bliss in the doing of God's will. No more pleading for the people of God to become involved. No more worrying if there is enough money to do God's will. Oh, the bliss in knowing God. There's nothing like it in the whole wide world.

"Blessed are the poor in spirit" — those who feel their spiritual need of God, those who sense their spiritual poverty, those who are humble and rate themselves as insignificant.

Oh, the bliss of those who know they are poor without God and need the King. They are kingdom people. Here ends the first lesson on the Beatitudes, the declarations of Jesus which build character.

VIII. Brokenhearted People

"Blessed are those who mourn, for they will be comforted" (Matthew 5:4).

Those who followed Jesus up the mountain were eager to hear his teachings. The idle and indifferent would not make the effort. Jesus does not begin his teaching with commands and demands. He begins with declarations. He talks about promises and blessings as he describes the very stuff of character.

Goethe gave us the tale of a wonderful silver lamp. He said when it was placed in a fisherman's hut, it changed the atmosphere of the hut — all within shined like silver. Jesus' beatitudes are like that lamp. Anyone embracing his teachings will have life lighted up.

A man I talked with had a pacer wedged under his skin near his right shoulder, a gadget connected to his heart by a couple of valves, designed to encourage his heart to pump blood more regularly. He told me the pacer cost him $15,000.

Obviously, of course, the pacer was worth it. Without it he might not live. How much you spend to keep alive is of little consequence under such circumstances. There is hardly anything you would not sacrifice if your life were hanging in the balance. That new automobile, that trip to the islands, that new television screen big as a room, that new house, that fat nest egg you have been tucking away for retirement all these years — all could be sacrificed for the sake of saving a life, whether it is your own or one of the members of your family. There just isn't enough money in the world to exchange for life. Is there anything you would exchange for life?

The man talked on and I discovered there was something he would exchange for his life. It wasn't the $15,000. It didn't have anything to do with money. I listened intently to him now. The suspense was almost too much to bear as I tried to catch what it was he would exchange his life for. It made me think of Jesus' story in the sixteenth chapter of Luke, the story of the rich man and the poor man, Lazarus, full of sores who pled to be fed, and how later the tables were turned, the rich man now in need and his desire to exchange everything for a cup of water. If the rich man had life to live over, knowing what he now knew, things would be different, he claimed. Ah, how circumstances change attitudes! Jesus said even if someone arose from the dead, some would not repent or come to God. They would continue to live out life the same old way. It is difficult to persuade a person who is well that not all is well.

By now the man showed pain in his features, not because the pacer wasn't working. It was. There was something else wrong with his heart; something had pierced him. The youngest of his three sons had been killed in an automobile accident. He was a tall, strapping fellow, bright-eyed with a sharp mind, "full of life," as we say, following in his father's footsteps, a future of real promise. The son was dead now.

The man's lips quivered as he spoke, eyes glued to the floor as he poured out his grief. He spoke more slowly: "I had heart trouble before my son's death. Naturally, the shock of his death had an effect on me. That's why they put this pacer under my skin." He looked directly at me, eyes revealing a brokenhearted father, as he continued: "You know, it should have been me who died. I would have gladly exchanged my life for his. I would give up this pacer in a moment if I could see him walk through that door." The man's head tuned toward a picture of the young man hanging on the wall. As he gazed at the picture, his hand moved almost automatically and came to rest over his heart.

The only thing I could think of saying to the man, a man whose heart had been pierced by sorrow, was this beatitude of Jesus, "Blessed are those who mourn, for they will be comforted." I felt inadequate for this occasion. A year had gone by since the young son died. Yet, the tenor of the man's voice was as if it had happened yesterday. The man put me at ease. He took his other hand and placed it on my shoulder. "Yes," he replied. "I think I know what you mean. Sorrow can be borne with the faith you proclaim."

His words hovered in my memory all that day and the next and the next. The faith we proclaim through the church of Our Lord is a blessed faith. It comforts those who are brokenhearted. It helps the brokenhearted to see more than death and to live on. There is even some value to sorrow, if it can be expressed that way. Sir Edward William Elgar, a largely self-taught English composer (1857-1934), once said of a promising young girl singer, "She will be great when something happens to break her heart." A new dimension comes to life for those who are brokenhearted, at least for those who permit God to show them more than death. The Almighty Father exchanged his Son to give life and courage to believers. There was courage on the ground where Mary stood brokenhearted, not crying, "Why? Oh, why?" but gaining strength from the words that came from her son on the cross.

There are other aspects to this subject of sorrow. In this age which desires instant happiness as readily as instant mashed potatoes, we can learn the value of discipline. Psychologist Stephen Goldbart and psychotherapist Joan DiFuria have noticed increasing psychological problems among some who have reaped riches from the high tech economy at a young age. They reported that "although their clients' wealth brought them comfort beyond their wildest dreams, it also brought a sense of isolation, uncertainty, and imbalance — as if they had been teleported into an alien world that was very pleasant at times but still completely strange." One person said it was difficult to talk with people about it. "Other people just think, 'Shut up! You have what everyone dreams of.' What they don't understand is that change is always difficult and sometimes it's painful" (*Los Angeles Times*, March 14, 2000).

So you see, we can become despondent and mourn over our plight in life, even when money is not a problem. We may try to take shortcuts, neglecting the discipline necessary to reach the goals which bring deeper happiness, and "cash in" on the immediate or obvious. But shortcuts seldom work. There is not much comfort in having achieved a goal without understanding what life is about. You cannot be great until something happens to your heart.

Since sorrow is a part of life, is not Jesus saying we need to become comforters? If we see suffering in the world and refuse to help, we become callous. If we see sin in the world and brush it off with a sigh, "That's the way things are these days," and fail to bring good into the world, we become world sick. And, if we cannot see our own sin for what it is, we cannot realize the presence of God who sheds a new light on life. "There is no light in us," as Paul would say it (1 Thessalonians 5). We need to be sorry for the suffering in the world, for humankind's injustices, and sorry for our own sins enough to despise them and want to be rid of them. We need to become comforters.

In *The Mayor Who Mastered New York*, Lately Thomas wrote, "As no other mayor ever had been, William J. Gaynor has been the father of his city; the people had trusted him. Instinctively, the throng of voiceless, uninfluential, disregarded citizens, periodically flattered and regularly exploited by those elected to power, had recognized that in Gaynor they had a mayor who was always, unequivocally and unalterably, on their side. This was unique. This was Gaynor."

Certainly this was and is Christ. He is humankind's Savior. He is our comforter. He is on our side. That is why he is so believable when he says, "Blessed are those who mourn, for they will be comforted."

People can be hurt deeply. But why should a widow or widower, for example, remain in the valley of the shadow of death while a dear one has already passed through? Why do some who sorrow refuse to be comforted?

I know why. I had to learn after my wife's death that "... bees gather the best honey from the bitterest herbs" and that "the darkest hour is nearest the dawn." There is a new dimension to life for those who are brokenhearted, but only for those who permit God to show them more than death.

God does not rejoice in sorrow. He is on our side. God rejoices in a person who sorrows for the right things.

False mourning brings no comfort: mourning over outward losses; lamenting when we cannot be satisfied. We can fall asleep in our own security. We can become earthly-minded. We can ignore applying the promises. We can slacken the strings of duty. We can have tears without Christ.

True mourning knows that the lancing of a wound is necessary before a cure. True mourning is for real — sanctifying, humbling, transporting, quieting, and abiding. We are never alone when we mourn. God is on our side and by our side. He provides character building.

Saint Basil said, "Holy mourning is the seed out of which the flowers of eternal joy doth grow."

In Mortensen's *Meister Eckart*, the wondrous beggar exclaims, "... would sooner be in hell and have God, than in heaven and not have him."

The man with the pacer and the lost son has a bad heart and a good faith. That's what counts. He taught me something about what is important, about what really matters, about values in life. He made the beatitude of Jesus on the brokenhearted a little more meaningful for me. I hope he has for you, too. Character begins to shine through brokenhearted people.

IX. Disciplined People

"Blessed are the meek, for they will inherit the earth" (Matthew 5:5).

A television quiz show would flash a word before a contestant and the contestant was expected to say the first word that came to mind. Psychologists have been known to use this technique. The matter of association reveals a certain amount of understanding of a subject.

If I flashed the word *Christ* before your eyes, you might well reply *cross*. It is impossible to think of Christ without a cross. Therefore, it would be natural for you to associate the word *cross* with *Christ.*

Now what is the first word that comes to your mind when I mention the word *meek*? Your response might be any one of these: weak, flabby, spineless, submissive, subservient, or indefensible.

Whatever your answer, the meaning of the word *meek* has such a varied and vast background that it almost defies translation.

The history of the word *meek* goes back to the Hebrews. It was a favorite word of the psalmist: "O Lord, you will hear the desire of the meek; you will strengthen their heart, you will incline your ear to do justice for the orphan and the oppressed so that those from earth may strike terror no more" (Psalm 10:17-18).

Jesus assuredly knew Psalm 10. In his beatitude, he takes a page from another psalm, "But the meek shall inherit the land, and delight themselves in abundant prosperity" (Psalm 37:1).

The Hebrew visualized the meek person as loving and obedient, gladly accepting the guidance of God. The Hebrew would contend that the meek person never becomes resentful or bitter. The meek would humbly accept what God gives in life. Such a life, therefore, would be strengthened as only a life of meekness could be, a life receptive to the beautification of God.

The word *meek* also has a Greek ancestry. It has reference to an animal which has been tamed or trained. For example, I used to have a Welsh Corgi named Squire. Every morning Squire thought he had to jump into the shower before I did. For some reason, he was obsessed with water. (It could be because he grew up with a swimming pool in his backyard!) He vigorously protested when I lifted him out of the shower. It took quite a few training sessions to teach him to sit outside the shower door while I took a shower. Now after Squire was trained to do that, the Greeks would say he was "under control." The Greek word *praus* for *meek* meant exactly that — "under control."

Aristotle, Greek philosopher of the fourth century B.C. (384-322 B.C.), one of the greatest thinkers of all time, went to great length explaining the meaning of something. The good-tempered person, Aristotle said, "... is angry with the right people, at the right things, in the right way ..." (*Nicomachean Ethics*, Book IV, 5, p. 373). In contrast, he called the bad tempered "... those who are angry at the wrong things, more than is right, and longer, and cannot be appeased until they inflict vengeance or punishment" (*Ibid.*)

In addition to this meaning, Greek thought considered the word *meek* as a form of gentleness when one has the right to be severe, such as a judge who could adhere to strict justice but tempers the sentence to justice with mercy within the law. Robert Browning, English poet (1812-1889), referred to the word *meek* as the person who has giant strength but does not try to use it as a giant. Thus, the meek person possesses both gentility and strength.

Combine these backgrounds of Hebrew and Greek describing the word *meek* and the result is a two-pronged concept: self-control and God-control.

Certainly self-control is needed. It is a matter of discipline. Church people in Lent exercise self-restraint, disciplining themselves in specific ways. Maybe some of the things given up for Lent need to be given up altogether! And, maybe some of the things we do for God during Lent need to be done all year!

Lack of self-control is a people hazard. For example, yearning for food every time we walk past the refrigerator. Or overspending, never satisfied until the "best of the line" is purchased.

Overspending can master us and our economic situation can become tenuous, threatening all that is dear to us. Some need to cut up a few plastic cards. We vow there is nothing in the world we would not do for our families, when it might be far better for them if some things were left undone.

Or, tempers rage until we become choleric people, ready to be angry at the drop of a hat. Everything and everyone irritates us when we know that the trouble lies within us and not with others. The release of frustrated anger can become a habit. We "blow a fuse," as some describe it.

These everyday occurrences can master us instead of our mastering them. For a free people, we surely do lose our freedom of choice rather easily. Overeating, overspending, and overindulgence in one's feelings are illustrations of how we can become mastered. That's why we have to have laws to protect ourselves from one another. Moreover, there are laws to protect ourselves from ourselves. We even have to write on some containers that the stuff can cause cancer.

We all need self-control. It seems difficult to fathom that the laws of God are for our own health and happiness. We can go to the other extreme and follow in the footsteps of the scribes and Pharisees Jesus talked about, so proud of our non-forming practices that the non-habit forming practices become gods. What this country needs, more than a curb on inflation, is a curb on self-will that is based on desires instead of needs.

How do we get under control? We all have free will, the nonbeliever as well as the believer. The nonbeliever can exercise self-control. The agnostic can exercise self-control by selecting the best choices in life. An agnostic can be very high on ethical choices. Agnostics have been known to be as moral as the next person. God has not penned up the human mind.

But the believer, self-control comes from beyond self, beyond personal choices, beyond likes and dislikes. The believer looks to God and not to self alone for strength. The believer submits to God's way of life for human beings. The believer exercises his faith and discovers self-control as well. The meek person trusts, obeys, and submits to God.

Job had this attitude: "... The Lord gave, and the Lord has taken away; blessed be the name of the Lord" (Job 1:21). Mary had this attitude: "Here am I, the servant of the Lord; let it be with me according to your word" (Luke 1:38). Paul had this attitude: "What am I to do, Lord?" (Acts 22:10). Jesus had this attitude: "My Father, if it be possible, let this cup pass from me; yet not what I want but what you want" (Matthew 26:39).

There is a place for selfless anger. When Jesus saw the moneychangers in the Temple, his eyes must have blazed with anger. The world would be far worse if it were not for the anger of a righteous person. The meek person has this character ingredient. Moses had it when he threw down the tablets in disgust over the people's idolatry. Jesus claimed it for himself, "Take my yoke upon you, and learn from me; for I am gentle (meek) and humble in heart, and you will find rest for your souls. For my yoke is easy, and my burden is light" (Matthew 11:29-30).

A God-controlled life inherits blessings. When Jesus said the "meek ... will inherit the earth," he was not talking about the meek ruling the earth or the meek owning the land. Jesus was talking about the now, not about some future promised land. Jesus assures us that the promises of God are for today. The person who is God-controlled has a feeling of security. The outward circumstances of life do not thwart or control such a person. The Christian is controlled by God. The Christian knows that no experience in life can separate a believer from God.

There is power within a meek person. When a person is controlled by God, the person has taken the first step to being under control.

In his biography of Robert Barclay, Elton Trueblood writes:

> *George Fox, a man of energy and courage, had grasped a great idea, the idea that Christian experience could be couched in the present tense. He was able to arouse men and women in a remarkable way by the direct question: "What canst thou say?" He discovered the power which always emerges when men move over from speculation to experience, and when they provide a*

verification of the reality of what they experience by the only evidence which is convincing, the evidence of changed lives.

A meek person is a changed person. A meek person has a great inheritance — abundant living.

I hope your reaction to the word *meek* is a little different now. If I flashed this word *meek* before you now, what words would come to your mind?

I hope these might be included: obedience, gentility, strength, courage, self-control, God-controlled, power, attitude, righteous anger, and God-experienced. When this beatitude of Jesus, "Blessed are the meek, for they shall inherit the earth," flashes across your mind, it is my hope you will commit yourself to the experience of a God-controlled life. If you do, you will inherit a present happiness which you have never known before. Disciplined people are like that. True character shines through.

X. Righteous People

"Blessed are those who hunger and thirst after righteousness, for they shall be satisfied" (Matthew 5:6).

Starvation was a real possibility in the locale and time of Jesus. Rarely did the Palestinian have meat to eat. Life was cheap. Starvation was not unusual. Furthermore, in that ancient world, water was not easily accessible. Wells and streams were often at great distances. It was not uncommon for water to be sold in the marketplace.

Food and water, the two basic necessities of life, were not taken for granted in Jesus' day. Our Lord knew what it meant to be hungry and thirsty, especially during his forty days in the wilderness. His humanity is very evident in this beatitude. He became one of us.

In the United States of America, most people do not have to worry about the availability of food and water. Our marketplaces have everything, wrapped in attractive packages. If Jesus took the twelve disciples through one of our supermarkets, they might joke with him, saying, "If we had all this food, it wouldn't have been necessary for you to multiply those fish and loaves of bread when you fed the multitude!" In fact, the Palestinian's eyes would have gotten bigger if he saw what is on our shelves for cats and dogs!

What a time to live! Yet, millions of people in the world go to bed hungry. Captured on television, the eyes of the starving, especially in poorly developed countries, haunt our insides. In this great agricultural land, it seems almost impossible that someone could be hungry. Nevertheless, parishes have requests every week from people who have need of food. Go to any downtown area in any city and you will see people holding out their cups for something to eat. The homeless and the hungry in this nation, in a time of affluence, are a blotch on our nation's record. Neither the politicians nor charitable institutions have figured out how to erase this need. Most national churches have raised millions of dollars to help feed the hungry across the world. Fortunately, some of this money is used to help nations develop agriculturally.

Jesus' beatitude about being hungry and thirsty for righteousness would be understood by the hungry. His words penetrated their experience.

Most of us do not know what it is like to be hungry. Or, maybe we do. We desire food from a different angle; not because of its unavailability but because it is readily available. The "Diet People" make billions off of millions of people who wish to lose weight. Fighting weight is a national pastime. Analysts say Americans are too fat. So, we do know something of that gnawing feeling, that empty feeling which is so hard to fight off. The desire for food which we know we do not need can almost drive a person insane.

We can appreciate more the feeling of Jesus' hearers when he talked about hungering and thirsting for a right relationship with God after contemplating our feelings about hunger for food and beverage.

Desire is an important factor in life. It can make the seemingly impossible possible. Desire can change situations. It can change lives. Desire can determine the outcome of events. Sportswriters love to write about teams, previously unbeaten, who are beaten by an apparently less talented team, a team which had the desire to win.

The old saying, "You get what you want," has a strand of truth in it. If you desire something earnestly enough, you are more likely to obtain it. If you want to achieve something higher than your present grasp, desire can be an extension of your grasp.

Desire has its demands, however. If you set out to reach some goal, and you really desire that goal, you may find yourself doing all kinds of unordinary things to reach that goal. The hours you may have to put in, the sacrifices you may have to make in order to achieve your goal become secondary. For reaching this goal of yours, the time and energy and sacrifice are not too high a price to pay.

Translate that feeling over into this beatitude of Jesus, for all this is involved. Our Lord knows about hunger and thirst; he also knew something about human desire. He knew that if a person really wants a right relationship with God, it would be granted. He knew that if a person really desires to serve God, the capacity to serve would be given. Thus, any church passionately desiring its pews filled for worship can realize more of its potential. Any church needing more funds to carry on the Lord's work will find funds readily available in the hearts of the believers. Any body of believers wanting justice exercised among people can be led to find ways of accomplishing it. With God all these things are possible. The question is: Do the people desire to love, trust, and obey God above everything? Settle that question and a great many of the problems in the world can be solved.

The rich ruler who came to Jesus wanted to know how to inherit eternal life. Jesus said he could start by keeping the commandments. The fellow said he had always kept the commandments, since his youth. Jesus got to the heart of the questioner by saying he lacked one thing. The fellow wanted to know what that was. Jesus was quick with the answer — share your wealth with the poor. The young man walked away. He didn't like the answer. He desired his wealth more than he desired God (Luke 18:18-25).

Another person wanted to follow Christ and Christ told him, "Foxes have holes, and birds of the air have nests; but the Son of Man has nowhere to lay his head." In other words, following Christ is not a Sunday school picnic. Two others were invited to follow Christ but gave lame excuses. They really didn't desire to follow Christ (Luke 9:57-62).

If you follow Christ, you may not have an easy road to travel. The question is: Are you willing to sacrifice yourself as Jesus sacrificed himself on the cross? Do you desire God that much?

Jesus told the disciples what they would have to do in order to follow him: "Whoever loves father or mother more than me is not worthy of me; and whoever loves son or daughter more than me is not worthy of me; and whoever does not take up the cross and follow me is not worthy of me. Those who find their life will lose it, and those who lose their life for my sake will find it" (Matthew 10:37-39). Is that what you desire? Do you desire God that much?

I think this scripture penetrated Martin Luther's mind as he wrote the hymn, "A Mighty Fortress Is Our God": "Were they to take our house, goods, honor, child, or spouse, though life be wrenched away, they cannot win the day. The Kingdom's ours forever" (*Lutheran Book of Worship*, No. 229).

There are demands as well as desires. You may desire God and not be willing to meet his demands. You cannot have God without the other. Some say they are interested in God. That's nice. But, are they willing to say with Paul, "For to me, living is Christ ..." (Philippians 1:21).

Some say they will worship and become more active in the Christian church some time. Christ says, "But the hour is coming, and is now here ..." (John 4:23).

Our response to the demands of God indicates whether or not we truly desire God. Our response is a barometer which reveals the temperature of a Christian. John observed in the book of Revelation that the church in Laodicea was "... neither cold nor hot" (Revelation 3:15).

Christianity is not for the dilettante, the part-time lover of God who considers religion a pastime. Christianity is not even for those who claim membership in a church but whose church has no claim on them, for they shrink from any demands put on them or withdraw, if only momentarily, when they surmise too much is expected of them.

Christianity is for those whose faith begins with a cross and the sacrifice it entails in following this Jesus of the cross. Christianity is for believers who comprehend they are a part of the body of Christ and not the possessors of a private religion. We are not really volunteers in the life of our Lord's church; we are all God's ministers. In the *Lutheran Book of Worship* (p. 165) in the Suffrages we pray, "Clothe your ministers with righteousness." This means everybody. To "clothe" does not mean by Hart, Schaffner, and Marx, but to take on the role of a person responsible to God for what is going on or not going on in the world God loves so much.

Christianity is for those who hunger and thirst for a personal relationship with God and his creation, which simultaneously makes them agents of God's work of reconciliation. We cannot play games with God. We can't play church. This is a matter of life and death, a matter of joyfully appropriating the demands of God. The Christian can be satisfied with no less a life.

There is a lot of dissatisfaction in the world. A man shot himself and his children because he couldn't stand living any longer without his wife who died of cancer. He asked not to be condemned for taking the lives of his children since he had brought them into the world. Because of his personal dissatisfaction, he played God for a few minutes with a gun in his hand instead of a cross. What we are dissatisfied about tells something about our desires.

Have you heard the story of the Pastor's Dream? The pastor had a dream about the disciples and Paul. The disciples and Paul were together, and Peter began to talk about retirement. Peter said he was offered a new boat and new tackle and a house by the shore. He was a little tired of going around preaching, and furthermore, not many people took seriously what he said anyway. Matthew said he was thinking of retirement, too. His books were not selling, and the royalties were few. He had been offered a position as Chief of the Income Tax Bureau. Matthew thought they had made him an offer which he could not refuse. Paul said that Aquila and Priscilla had offered to set him up in the tent-making business. He said he was tired of being a traveling evangelist, and the pace was giving him ulcers. He said he thought he had suffered enough ... Then Andrew spoke. "But, remember, Peter, when Jesus asked, 'Do you love me?' What would he say to you now? Remember when he stilled the storm? And Matthew, remember when the wind blew in the Upper Room? Remember, Paul, what you experienced on the road to Damascus?" There was a silence, and then one by one they replied: Peter: "Guess I really didn't have my heart set on that kind of fishing after all." Matthew: "Being Chief of the Income Tax Bureau isn't the best job in the world." Paul, turning to go, said, "See you next time around fellows, when we talk about our journeys, for the answer is blowing in the wind."

It was only a dream. But, what is your dream? Do you desire God more than going fishing or holding some important position? Do you desire God more than retirement? Are you tired of well-doing?

This beatitude of Jesus gets at the heart of our appetite. Jesus makes a promise. He said if you desire God enough to meet the demands of our living God, you will be satisfied. There is satisfaction in knowing that you have a right relationship with God, the satisfaction of mercy, peace, and love. There is satisfaction in desiring what is right for yourself and what is right for others. There is satisfaction in paying the price of loving and trusting and obeying God above everything. There is satisfaction in being dissatisfied with the way things are the way they are, dissatisfied with injustices perpetuated through the ages, and then doing something about them, even putting your life on the line for the things God desires. If you have an appetite for the things of God, you will be satisfied. There is no better food for the starving soul. It is a matter of character.

XI. Kindhearted People

"Blessed are the merciful, for they will receive mercy" (Matthew 5:7).

The beatitudes have a rhythm about them. Jesus states a truth and doubles back with emphasis. The poor in spirit get to know God; those who mourn are comforted; the meek have an inheritance; the hungry and thirsty are satisfied.

I like what Alexander Maclaren in his *Expositions Of Holy Scripture* wrote about the beatitudes: "It is the application in detail of the great principle which our Lord endorses in its Old Testament form when he said that the first great commandment, the love of God, had a companion consequent on and like unto it, the love of our neighbor. Religion without beneficence, and beneficence with religion, are equally maimed. The one is a root without fruit, and the other a fruit without a root" ("The Gospel According to Matthew," p. 144). For the young in heart, the word "beneficence" means "beneficial" or an "act of kindness."

In this beatitude we come to the word *mercy* and the doubling back with the emphasis that those who have mercy as a part of their personality fabric experience mercy.

The word *mercy* has varied meanings in both the Old and the New Testaments. In the Old Testament, God's mercy is shown in forgiveness when Israel is restored, in the deliverance of the chosen people from their enemies, in the fulfillment of a promise, in the gathering of the exiled people and their return, the provision made for them in the wilderness, in the restoration of communication between God and his people. God's mercy or compassion or pity, in the Old Testament, is based upon a covenant relationship with the people. God made a promise to be with Israel. The Hebrews had a *mercy seat*, a slab of refined gold about seven feet by three and a half feet on top of the Ark of the Covenant. It was not a lid or covering for the ark. It was a support for other parts of the ark. The *mercy seat* was sprinkled with blood on the Day of Atonement. They felt their need of God's mercy.

Furthermore, in the Hebrew family, *mercy* was an integral part of their life. Mercy — help, love, need — was a duty. Mercy made a family. Without mercy, there was no such thing as a family. That's not a bad idea. We might take a tip or two from them about what really makes a family.

This same idea was reflected in their community life. They took care of the children, the aged, the poor, the parentless, and the widows. In some of the epistles in the New Testament this thought is lifted up. They believed that without this communal concern and aid they would be a helpless and destitute nation. One of the worst failings of a conqueror, they felt, would be to disregard the poor and the needy.

Of course, there are numerous examples in the Old Testament wherein mercy was lacking. It was not only in dealing with the people they defeated in battle but in judicial matters. An idolator, for example, was shown no mercy. The murderer and the false witness were seldom given mercy.

In the New Testament, acts of mercy were a part of the fiber of Jesus' ministry. Numerous accounts describe his acts of healing, his concern for the plight of people. Jesus desired each person to be whole. He took special interest in the blind, the leper, the helpless, and the hungry. When Jesus spoke this beatitude about mercy, he was speaking from experience.

God's mercy has been shown in countless ways. Barren Elizabeth was given the gift of a child. Persecutor Paul was given new life. Ailing Epaphroditus was healed (Philippians 2:27). The list never ends.

There were instances in the Old Testament life whereby mercy was extended only to "their kind of people." Our country's history is deluged with this same malady. Jesus taught that no matter who they be — rich or poor, Jew or Gentile, scribe or Pharisee, tax collector or sinner — we are to be merciful. We are to show kindness.

But we miss the central thrust of this word *mercy* if we only think of it as having pity upon those who deserve to be punished.

We are not called upon to play the role of God, giving somebody "a break," when we know the person is undeserving. The mercy Jesus spoke about and illustrated is not a haughty attitude toward others, condescending in our attitude. It isn't hard to be kind when you can "afford to be," we say. Jesus might agree. Jesus didn't waste much time on people who got "their kicks" out of being good, good only for self-gratification and to prompt others to think well of them. He said they would have their "reward." And, Jesus was not talking about a negative attitude, a willingness to suspend judgment or to mitigate justifiable severity. Jesus was talking about a quality of life for the Christian, a positive attitude toward life. Oh, the bliss of the kind heart! Character shines!

It is hard to imagine a kind heart in a negative person. It is difficult to see how a negative attitude toward life can result in kindness. Have you ever known a negative person to have a kind heart? Oh, the person may have flashes of kindness here and there. But, the negative cannot have kindness because negativism is a form of hatred.

Think of the life of Christ. We never think of Christ as negative. If a person was caught in sin, he didn't give up on the whole human race. He gave his life for humankind. If people tried to trick him by twisting his words, a favorite pastime of the scribes and Pharisees, he didn't let their negativism thwart him from pursuing his goal. Jesus became determined more than ever to go all the way to Jerusalem.

The scribes and Pharisees were basically negative people. That's why Jesus put them in their place more than once. They could not see any good coming out of a little "hick town" like Nazareth. As a consequence, nothing good came out of them. These negative people trumped up a false trial to get rid of Jesus. The negative get more joy out of pinning someone to a cross than they do out of crossing the road to help somebody who is bleeding to death. The negative are like hit-and-run drivers. They don't want to look back long enough to see what they have done. They must be on their way so they can condemn somebody else and cry, "Crucify him! Crucify him!" They are "fruit without root." They have no rhythm in their lives.

There was a preacher in Texas who reported on the results of a house call made by two laypersons of his church. They were greeted by a man with hair mussed up and a kind of wild look in his eyes. The laypersons told him they were visiting for the church and would like to talk with him about religion. He answered: "Oh, good heavens, I have so much trouble that I just cannot take on the church and religion in addition!" (Gerald Kennedy, *Pulpit Digest*, March, 1969, p. 57).

Think about what the man really said. The first thing that he mentioned was trouble. That's the first thing negative people always think about. He was so busy trying to bail himself out of trouble, whatever it might have been, that he could not listen to a possible solution. His hair was all mussed up. He didn't have time to take care of his appearance. He had a wild look in his eyes. He was afraid. God was something to be tacked on to his life, if he ever had the time. He couldn't recognize the solution to his troubles when the solution stood in his own doorway. Life was not a joy for him. He didn't believe anybody could have mercy on him. As a consequence, he did not have kindness in his own heart. In reality, he thought the world was a heartless place. Nobody was going to have mercy on him. Why should he have mercy on anybody? He never gave God a second thought. He was down at the marketplace on crucifixion day. He didn't even have time to see who was being crucified. On resurrection day, he was still at his old stand. He didn't need God. All he needed was to get rid of his troubles. If he could get rid of them, then he would start living. Little did he know that the positive, the kind, the merciful have plenty of troubles. Not everything is "sweetness and light" for the kindhearted. But the difference is they never grow bitter. They never become negative over a 24-hour period. They see mercy ahead.

The kindhearted life is the life Jesus commended. There are not enough kindhearted people to go around in this world of merciless killings of the human spirit.

What effect does this attitude of mercy, this attitude of kindness, have upon a person? For one thing, it prompts a person to be merciful in the judgment of other people. The kindhearted are not eager to think the worst. The kindhearted put the most charitable construction upon others' actions, as Luther taught in his catechism. The kindhearted are more understanding of the circumstances, situations, and factors involved in other lives. We need such understanding in our businesses, homes, schools, and churches.

Another effect is that the kindhearted see their own need of mercy, their own need of God, their own failures to love God and others. We who pray for forgiveness would become despondent if God treated us like we sometimes treat others!

Try being more kindly, more merciful for the next week and you will see something good happen in your own life. In the face of weakness and wickedness, try being merciful. In the face of hatred and injustice, try mercy. Discover the power of patient kindness. Be gentle. Return good for evil. Help transform others. Be transformed yourself, as Paul suggested in Romans 12.

When you do this, you will be surprised to recognize your own need of God. Kindheartedness will teach you to be charitable with others. In addition, you will be given the power to deal with antagonisms. For the root of mercy is in God. This rhythm in life will become a part of you so that you can deal with the low points as well as the high points in life.

Someone asked a scholar: "Why is it that you study so slowly but pray so very fast?" "Because," sighed the sage, "when I pray, I am talking to God; but when I study, God is talking to me."

In this beatitude, Jesus is talking to us. He is beckoning us to study the subject of mercy. God is saying something to each of us in this matter of acquiring the kind heart. Kindheartedness gives rhythm to life. Kindheartedness adds a needed and unique quality to the fabric of our personalities. Mercy is character in action.

XII. Pure-In-Heart People

"Blessed are the pure in heart, for they will see God" (Matthew 5:8).

Time elapsed between Jesus' transfiguration on a mountain and his triumphal entry into Jerusalem. Back on the mountain where he gave three disciples an experience they would never forget, victory was in the air! Proclaim truth and people will embrace it. That was his hope.

It seemed verified as he rode on the back of that donkey amidst the cheers and palm branches. Now the city of Jerusalem took notice of him. Before the week was out, he would be the talk of the town. He had once said, "Every kingdom divided against itself is laid waste, and no city or house divided against itself will stand" (Matthew 12:25). Even as he looked into the eyes of those who waved palm branches, he knew there would be those who would stand against him. As he rode along, imagine him repeating to himself these words of this beatitude, "Blessed are the pure in heart, for they will see God." The people of Jerusalem had the privilege craved by generations — they could see God. "Tell the daughters of Zion, Look, your king is coming to you, humble, and mounted on a donkey ..." (Matthew 21:5).

But Jesus said no one could see God unless the person had a pure heart. Jerusalem, like all of us, needed a pure heart. As the week grew older, Jerusalem's impurity became visible as a cross was thrust into the ground. Only the hearts of impure people could nail Purity to a piece of wood, stick it in the ground, and leave him to die.

For a clearer understanding of Jesus' thoughts as he made his way into Jerusalem, for a fuller appreciation of his beatitude on purity, again we must go back to the Old Testament.

Purity (*katharos*) had its roots in ritual observance. Certain animals were considered unclean or impure for sacrifice (Leviticus

11). Only the best could be offered to God. This same concept applied to the human body. If a person touched a dead body, the person was considered unclean or impure for seven days (Numbers 19:11-13). When a religious man of the Old Testament sat down to eat, he did not go to the table until he had washed his hands in a certain way. It was not only because of the fear of germs; it was a religious ritual. The ceremony of purity was accomplished by holding each hand with fingers pointed up and pouring water over them until the water reached the wrist. Then each palm was cleansed by rubbing it with the fist of the other. Finally, the hands with fingers pointed downward; water was again poured down the hands and over the fingers. All this was religious ceremony prior to sitting down to eat. The next time somebody in your household complains about washing their hands before eating, try this ritual on them! Then they might not mind washing their hands in the usual way, before sitting down to dinner.

If you think this ritual is complicated, pity the High Priest on the Day of Atonement. He had to wash his whole body in clean water five times, and his hands and feet ten times! Such a ceremony made him pure and prepared him to officiate at the sacrifice on this most solemn of all Hebrew ceremonies. It was the day the priest, after cleansing, robed in linen garments, made atonement for all by killing the "bullock of the sin-offering," selected the scapegoat, confessed the transgressions of Israel over his head, and then sent the goat out into the wilderness of Judaea, carrying the people's sin "into a solitary land." That's how they felt they got rid of sin. And, that is how we got the name "scapegoat."

As an aside, when a pastor celebrates the Sacrament of The Lord' Supper, the hands are washed before touching the elements. This is a practice which goes back to this Old Testament ritual of purification, and secondarily, a matter of good hygiene.

Another consideration in this matter of understanding the word *purity*, in addition to ceremonial law, was the way priests were selected. In order to become a priest, one had to be a descendant of Aaron, something like the apostolic succession exercised by the Roman Catholic Church and Episcopal Church, and what Lutherans recently dealt with in negotiations with the Episcopal Church, the matter of accepting one another's clergy by apostolic succession. In the Old Testament, a person might be a scoundrel, but if he was a descendant of Aaron, he could become a priest. The most sainted man in the world could not become a priest unless he was a descendant of Aaron. The only thing which could prevent a descendant of Aaron from becoming a priest was to flunk the physical test. The Law laid down 142 physical blemishes, any one of which could disqualify a candidate.

All of this the Hebrew thought about when Jesus spoke on the phrase, "pure in heart." Jesus thought it was far more important to discover what is in a person's heart than this matter of externals or genealogy according to the Law.

The point of Jesus was not to condemn the outward religious observance. There is much to be said for the churchgoer, the Bible reader, the pray-er, the devout, the doer, the tither, and all the rest. The nonbeliever or casual believer seems to get a special "kick" out of watching churchgoers' demeanor on Sunday in contrast to the rest of the week, and sometimes justly so. But Jesus' point is a case for self-examination which leads inevitably to humiliation, and in turn leads a person to see the things of God. There is no way to purify other than seeing things God's way.

In the springime, gardeners are on their knees planting annuals. Where I walk with my dog, there is a man always out in his yard. I call him "Mr. Gardener Supreme." He likes that. He knows flowers by name, even the ones hard to pronounce. When he plants, he knows how tall they will be and what they will be like. He knows when they will bloom. He knows the care it takes to make a flower garden. A visitor to his flower garden may enjoy the beauty of it, but unless the visitor, too, knows something about the flowers, the visitor cannot see everything there is to be seen. You have to see things through the eyes of a flower gardener before you can see things his way.

Put it another way. It is awe-inspiring to see rockets launch courageous people into space. I remember when they were flying around the moon at Christmas time. They described what they saw and brought back pictures for the world to see. The greatest insight that came from that trip to the moon was a reading of the first ten verses of Genesis: "In the beginning God created the heavens and the earth ... And God said, 'Let there be light;' and there was light." A great part of the world, even the non-believing world, began to see things their way. Colonel Frank Borman said, "For about an hour, while we were on the back side of the moon, we were out of contact with the earth. It was an eerie feeling. When we came around into the light again, there was the earth, seeming to rise up out of darkness" (*Guideposts*, April, 1969). He also said there were 34 letters of complaint about their reading the Bible, but there were almost 100,000 letters telling them how meaningful it was. Most people saw it their way: "When we came around into the light again, there was the earth, seeming to rise up out of darkness."

Purity is a matter of light, seeing things God's way. What Jesus saw in the eyes of the people of Jerusalem was first light and then darkness, with his back on a cross.

If you and I will see what Jesus saw, we will see our own need of purity, our own need of light. Jesus said, "You are the light of the world." Oh, if we only were!

Frederick Buechner, in *The Hungering Dark*, wrote there are basically two ways to live out life. "The first, exemplified by an article written by one of the actresses in *The Persecution And Assassination Of Marat*, as performed by the inmates of the Asylum of Charenton under the direction of the Marquis de Sade. She told how some of the cast became ill before or after each performance '... after each new enactment of a murder by madmen and imbeciles, led by a fiend.' " Said Buechner: "And surely this is a kind of symbol of one of the ways that the world waits through its darkness, which is to lust after the very darkness that makes us sick, to revel in our despair, to smack our lips over our own vomit. This is one way to wait, and it is a tempting way because it makes us seem brave and indeed requires a kind of bravery — laughing in the face of the idiot light. It is tempting also because sometimes despair is easier than faith.

"The other way," says Buechner, "is to say, 'Hallelujah,' which means 'Praise God.' Praise God because the dark is never the end, the end is light, and the light has already broken through into the world out of the very heart of the world's darkness, which is the cross of the world's suffering. And it will break through again, as surely as, far off down the road, the rider comes again his weary, lonesome way" (Buechner, p. 111).

The rider comes again on Palm Sunday with a beatitude on his lips, "Blessed are the pure in heart, for they will see God." When you see things God's way, you are purified and you see light ahead. When the rider rides into your heart, light rises out of darkness. It is a matter of character.

XIII. Peacemaker People

"Blessed are the peacemakers, for they will be called children of God" (Matthew 5:9).

Indexes of books have always fascinated me. Whenever I look in an index, I think of the work someone has done to put in alphabetical order the subjects dealt with in a book; that is, I used to marvel at that accomplished task. Now, computers have taken over the job. Nevertheless, indexes still fascinate me.

They intrigue me most not by the subjects listed, but by the subjects omitted. I am always amazed how an author can write an entire book without mentioning a certain topic or word. For example, there are books on theology, the study of God, which never mention the word *prayer*. I don't understand how a person can write a book on the study of God without talking to God. Or, as a student of history, I have always appreciated the work of Arnold J. Toynbee and his wife Veronica. Yet, I cannot understand how Toynbee could have written a whole book on *A Study Of History* without mentioning the word *peace*. They wrote in great detail concerning their thesis that there is a rhythm in the histories of civilization, how certain patterns develop in the growth and breakdown of civilizations. I have possessed a copy of their book since May 26, 1948, and I still can't understand how they could have left out the word *peace* in a study of humankind. So, the subjects omitted in book indexes never cease to amaze me.

The oddity is not confined to book writing. Everyday conversations are monotonous, at times. We ask each other, "How are you?" without having the least intention of listening to the answer. We talk about the weather, as if some new phenomenon has arisen on the horizon that must be dealt with. We make small talk to keep the conversation flowing. We talk about what others are doing wrong without trying to be constructive. We talk about ourselves as if nobody else has problems. It is what we don't say that is amazing. Serious conversation on subjects that matter have a way of escaping us. We talk about the externals without talking about the eternals. What we don't say to each other in a serious way is rather amazing.

There are some words that cannot be omitted from life — death, for instance. When somebody dies, we often say, "He passed away." Pray tell, where did he go? Why are we so afraid to say the word *death*? Do we think it will go away if we don't mention it? He is dead, awaiting the resurrection to life or the resurrection to damnation (John 5:29). There is nothing you or I can do about it. It is done. It is finished. The dead man made his choice while he lived. The results will not go up on the board until resurrection day, not Easter, but the last day of civilization, whenever that is.

What we don't say about a dead person is probably a good thing. By the conversations I have heard at funerals, however, there never was a bad guy buried. The preacher is always expected to say something nice about the deceased, hard pressed as the preacher might be. We omit words about humankind being a failure and needing a victorious Christ. Death has a way of burying evil with it, or so we think. Seldom do we learn any lessons from those who mourn. There are just too many unsaid words. We dwell more on the attributes of the deceased than on the attributes of his God, if he had one.

I wonder what they said about Christ when he died on the cross? He wasn't an old man dying from cancer. He wasn't a man who needed a transplant. He was a young man full of life who became full of death in a matter of a few horrendous hours. What did they say about him? A captain in the Roman army, who assuredly was accustomed to seeing people die, was affected by Christ's demeanor on the cross and was heard to say, "Truly this man was God's Son!" (Matthew 27:54). Where did the captain get this expression "God's Son"? He was an emperor worshiper. The captain might as well have said, "He was a good man." One of the other Gospels reported the captain as saying, "Certainly this man was innocent!" (Luke 23:47). Regardless of how it is translated, the thought conveyed is, "He was a good man."

Was there no one else to speak about this man who hung lifeless on a cross other than a captain of the army? Mary, what did you say? Mary Magdalene, what did you say? Simon of Cyrene, what did you say? Peter, James, and John, wherever you were, what did you say? My goodness! Was there only an army captain to say anything except, "He was a good man"? Fifty days had to go by before anybody got enough courage to face the world and tell it like it was, "You are the Israelites, listen to what I have to say: Jesus of Nazareth, a man attested to you by God with deeds of power, wonders, and signs that God did through him among you, as you yourselves know — this man, handed over to you according to the definite plan and foreknowledge of God, you crucified and killed by the hands of those outside the law" (Acts 2:22-23). It took Peter fifty days to get over the shock of the crucifixion and the unbelievable resurrection to tell anybody about it.

Words of great people do not die with them. What they pass on in ways of wisdom aid generation after generation. We have learned that from sages of the past.

The words of Christ from the cross have been imbedded deeply in the minds of people for centuries. What he said on a mountainside will be contemplated for years to come. Whatever else we say about Christ, we have to say he was a peacemaker. "Blessed are the peacemakers, for they will be called children of God." Even a Roman captain saw in the Christ of the cross a peacemaker. "Truly this man was God's Son!"

We can get pretty excited about this subject of *peace*. There are many peace lovers; there are few peacemakers. What our country would give for a peacemaker these days! Nuclear weapons have not made the world safe for democracy, or safe period. A few years ago some senators and congressmen were eagerly preparing bills to establish a new department in our government, a Department of Peace. They claimed that a Secretary of Peace could pursue this matter of peace in the world with the same energy and dedication as people of science struggled to put somebody on the moon. They felt a great urgency to establish peace in the world for all time. Nobody could argue that point, but it didn't happen. We have a Department of War but we do not have a Department of Peace.

We can say this about Jesus in this matter of peacemaking. He had more in mind than people getting along with one another, more in mind than nations learning to live on a planet in some kind of harmony. He certainly was concerned for peace among nations, as he believed the people should "Give ... to the emperor the things that are the emperor's ..." (Matthew 22:21). However, he believed that peace with God had priority. Since Adam and Eve, humankind has been more at war with God than with one another. This is verified throughout history. At times, people would mold a golden calf to demonstrate their defiance, insisting that God shape up and pay more attention to his creation. At times, people would argue the existence of God and exalt the human mind. At times, people would claim to be God, acclaiming themselves more than mortal, as with Roman emperors. At times, people would assert God is outmoded or dead. At times, people would simply ignore God in the pursuit of their own happiness. Humankind has never found it difficult to wage war against God.

Jesus endeavored to show humans that God was not their enemy, although they hung him on a cross in an attempt to disprove it. Jesus sprung back to life to show human beings that their real enemy, their last enemy, death, had been destroyed.

The role of Jesus Christ is peacemaker. The word *peace* means *completeness* or *wholeness*. We can think of peace in terms of *reconciliation*. When we are reconciled to God, when we are willing to accept life as the Creator intended, we become complete, whole. You cannot be a whole or complete person without God. This is not possible. That's why the nonbeliever or the partial believer never experience completeness or wholeness.

All of us, at one time or another, have tried to eliminate the word *death* from the index of our lives. We pretend it isn't there, except on forcible occasions. We embrace the attitude, in one form or another, that this is the only life there is. We almost never expect to die. Therefore, we become forever frustrated about life. We are torn between daring to live and fearing to die. Or, we may lose all hope of seeing anything ahead and want to get life over as quickly as possible. Or, we may want life never to end so much that we never permit ourselves to love anybody.

A neighbor of mine didn't want any more pets. He loved the pets of the other neighbors. He didn't want any of his own because, he told me, "I will become too attached to them and when they die, it will be like losing a child." He missed the joy of loving his own pet and having his own pet love him because he was afraid of being hurt. He knew that to love means you are going to be hurt some time. He didn't want that to happen to him again.

But that is exactly what happened to Jesus Christ. It will happen to anybody who loves the world so much that they give themselves for the completeness and wholeness of others. Because Christ was not only a peacemaker, he makes peacemakers of others. It is the one word that we need in our lives, as well as the word *death*. When you die and others look into your book of life, the word *peacemaker* needs to be in there.

John Glenn, the senator, went up into space again in 1998 on a mission to provide scientists information about the effects of age. When he was launched into space as the first American astronaut, news people inquired about his thoughts and fears as he shot through space with the real possibility of death as a result. Glenn replied calmly, "My peace had been made with my Maker for a number of years...." I rather imagine he cherished the same thought the second time he was launched into space.

Christ's resurrection has made it possible for us to be at peace with our Maker. He has also made it possible for us to launch out as peacemakers. In a real sense, the Christian church is God's "Department of Peace." It is God's way of assuring humankind that after a crucifixion there is always a resurrection. "Blessed are the peacemakers, for they will be called (sons and daughters) children of God." Peacemakers are people of character.

The beatitudes are building blocks for character: kingdom people, brokenhearted people, disciplined people, righteous people, kindhearted people, pure-in-heart people, and peacemaker people. The utilization of the beatitudes enables people to draw from truths that last forever and ever. They are character builders.

This matter of character building is a lifelong endeavor. Jesus bade us to be "perfect," but we know that is not possible for humankind. It is his way of encouraging us to follow him by including ingredients of character that make life purposeful and meaningful. Laws (the ten commandments) and Declarations (the beatitudes) help us latch onto principles that never die. They help us live with a sense of character.

www.ingramcontent.com/pod-product-compliance
Lightning Source LLC
Chambersburg PA
CBHW071732040426
42446CB00011B/2328